# MICROBITES
# MUMMIES
## RIVETING READS FOR CURIOUS KIDS

By
John Malam

Consultants
Dr. Joann Fletcher, Peter Chrisp

D0002820

## Second Edition

### DK Delhi

**Senior Editor** Sreshtha Bhattacharya
**Senior Art Editor** Vikas Chauhan
**Editor** Upamanyu Das
**Art Editor** Sanya Jain
**Managing Editor** Kingshuk Ghoshal
**Managing Art Editor** Govind Mittal
**Senior DTP Designers** Neeraj Bhatia,
Shanker Prasad
**Pre-Production Manager** Balwant Singh
**Production Manager** Pankaj Sharma

### DK London

**Senior Editor** Sam Atkinson
**US Editor** Kayla Dugger
**US Executive Editor** Lori Cates Hand
**Managing Editor** Lisa Gillespie
**Managing Art Editor** Owen Peyton Jones
**Production Editor** Gillian Reid
**Senior Production Controller** Meskerem Berhane
**Jacket Designer** Akiko Kato
**Jacket Design Development Manager**
Sophia MTT
**Publisher** Andrew Macintyre
**Associate Publishing Director** Liz Wheeler
**Art Director** Karen Self
**Publishing Director** Jonathan Metcalf

## First Edition

**Project Editor** David John
**Project Art Editor** Joanna Pocock
**Senior Editor** Fran Jones
**Senior Art Editor** Marcus James
**Category Publisher** Jayne Parsons
**Senior Managing Art Editor** Jacquie Gulliver
**Picture Researchers** Angela Anderson, Nicole Kaczynsky, Bridget Tilley
**Production** Erica Rosen
**DTP Designers** Matthew Ibbotson, Louise Paddick

This American Edition, 2020
First American Edition, 2001
Published in the United States by DK Publishing
1450 Broadway, Suite 801, New York, NY 10018

A catalog record for this book is available from the Library of Congress.
ISBN 978-1-4654-9735-2 (Paperback)
ISBN 978-1-4654-9844-1 (Hardcover)

DK books are available at special discounts when purchased in bulk
for sales promotions, premiums, fund-raising, or educational use.
For details, contact: DK Publishing Special Markets,
1450 Broadway, Suite 801, New York, NY 10018
SpecialSales@dk.com

Printed and bound in the UK

## A WORLD OF IDEAS:
### SEE ALL THERE IS TO KNOW

**www.dk.com**

# CONTENTS

# INTRODUCTION

Mummies, more than any other type of human remains, have the power to open windows to lost worlds—and none more so than the mummies of ancient Egypt. These preserved people are unique pieces of evidence. They're not the oldest mummies in the world, nor are they always the best preserved, but they're the ones that cast the greatest spell over us.

Egyptian mummies were the product of an age-old human desire—to survive death and allow the soul to live forever by preventing the body's decay. Whether this ever succeeded, no one can say, but one thing's certain—the fascination with mummies has kept them alive in the popular imagination.

When we study past civilizations, we tend to look at

THE WORLD WENT MUMMY-MAD WITH THE DISCOVERY OF TUTANKHAMUN'S TOMB IN 1922.

the remains of their monuments, writing, and other objects that have survived. But the mummy of a person who died long ago is often far more interesting than anything else an archaeologist might dig up. The reason for this is simple: a person who lived and died in the past can help piece together the past. Their bones,

ANUBIS, THE JACKAL-HEADED GOD OF EMBALMING, ANOINTS A YOUNG MAN.

teeth, flesh, vital organs, skin, hair, and fingernails hold amazing secrets about the time and place in which they lived. Today, advances in modern technology—such as X-rays, radiocarbon dating, and DNA analysis—are allowing us to unravel some of these mysteries for the first time.

This book tells the story of ancient Egypt and its mummies. You'll find out about the Egyptians' everyday lives, their strange gods, magic beliefs, and powerful pharaohs. You'll be guided through their massive stone buildings—their pyramids, temples, and tombs. You'll also discover how the Egyptians perfected the art of embalming and how their mummies can help us understand one of the greatest civilizations the world has ever known.

Thanks to the Egyptian practice of preserving their dead, we can still look into the faces of some of the most famous rulers of the ancient world, such as Tutankhamun and Ramesses the Great.

John Malam

# WHAT IS A MUMMY?

**Y**ou've probably opened this book because you want to find out the grisly truth about mummies. But which mummies are those, exactly? Are they the ones from Egypt or China, from South America or northern Europe? The fact is that mummies come from all over the world; it just happens that the ones from ancient Egypt are the most famous of them all.

THIS COFFIN CONTAINED THE MUMMY OF AN EGYPTIAN PRIESTESS.

## Preserved people

At one time, every mummy was a flesh-and-blood person— a living human being. One day, that person curled up his or her toes and died. Throughout human history, in every civilization on Earth, dead bodies have been buried in the ground, where they became worm food. Others were burned until they turned to ash. But a small number of bodies have been preserved.

It may sound creepy, but some ancient corpses, which can be thousands of years old, look so fresh that you'd think they were asleep. For them, time has stood still. For us, they're time capsules. Mummified people open a window to the past, and through them we can learn about the societies they came from. It is as if their voices can be heard again, speaking to us from long ago.

**Mummified by accident**

Most mummies in ancient Egypt were deliberately made. The Egyptian embalmers wanted to make their customers'

TOLLUND MAN WAS FOUND IN A PEAT BOG IN DENMARK. HE DIED ABOUT 2,400 YEARS AGO.

# BODIES HAVE BEEN FROZEN, DRIED OUT, EVEN PICKLED!

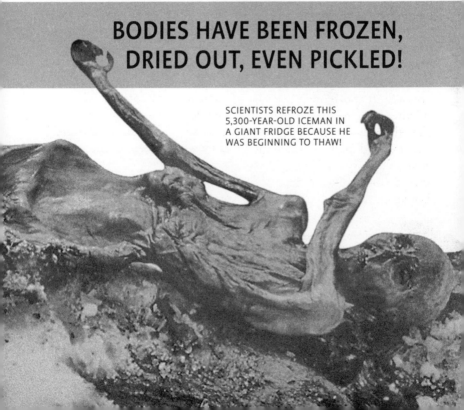

SCIENTISTS REFROZE THIS 5,300-YEAR-OLD ICEMAN IN A GIANT FRIDGE BECAUSE HE WAS BEGINNING TO THAW!

dead bodies last forever. But elsewhere in the world, some bodies became mummies by accident—there was no special embalming (preserving) treatment for them.

You probably wouldn't think of looking in a glacier or a peat bog to find a mummy. But it's in these unlikely places that some of the most magnificent mummies have been found.

## Ice man and bog man

In 1991, tourists found the dried-out body of a man frozen in a glacier on a mountain between Austria and Italy. He died in this bleak place 5,300 years ago, and the ice preserved him like meat in a freezer.

Bodies can even be preserved in places that contain very little oxygen, like marshy bogs. It's oxygen that makes flesh rot and iron rust.

The people who lived in northern Europe about 2,000 years ago didn't know this.

IN PERU, MUMMIES WERE BURIED IN A SQUATTING POSITION. THIS HELPED PRESERVE THEM, ALLOWING BODILY FLUIDS TO DRAIN DOWNWARD, OUT OF THE BODY.

They threw sacrifice victims and criminals into peat bogs. The conditions in these cold, airless, watery places were perfect for pickling bodies— their skin turned into leather. Peat cutters have found these bog bodies in England, Germany, and Denmark.

the skin from their dead and remove the internal organs. When a body was dry, it was "rebuilt" with sticks, reeds, animal hair, paste, and paint. The end result was a stuffed and painted mummy that looked more like a doll than a person.

## The first mummy makers

The ancient Egyptians were not the first people to mummify their dead.

That claim to fame belongs to the people of southern Peru and northern Chile, who, 10,000 years ago, began to bury corpses in the sand of the Atacama Desert. It was there, in one of the world's driest places, that human tissue was first mummified naturally by the environment. When the local people found that their loved ones were not rotting in the ground, they developed methods of artificial mummification. From about 5000 BCE, they began to strip

**WEIRD WORLD**

IN 2016, JOHN TORRINGTON'S SHIP, HMS *TERROR*, WHICH WENT MISSING IN 1845, WAS DISCOVERED ON THE ARCTIC SEABED. IT WAS AS PERFECTLY PRESERVED AS TORRINGTON'S BODY.

## Mummies in Asia

Deserts in other parts of the world have also produced "crops" of mummies.

TORRINGTON, AN ENGLISH SAILOR, WAS BURIED ON AN ARCTIC ISLAND IN 1846. HIS CREWMATES DUG A 5-FT (1.5-M) DEEP GRAVE FOR HIM IN THE PERMAFROST.

In China's Taklamakan Desert, there is a cemetery that was in use for 1,500 years, from about 1800 BCE to 300 BCE. The dried-out bodies found there have puzzled scientists, because they look like European people, not Asian. Who were they? What were they doing there? The answer seems to be that they were settlers who had traveled to Asia from Europe. No one knew anything about them until their well-preserved mummies were found.

MODERN SCIENCE USES ULTRA-LOW TEMPERATURES TO PRESERVE HUMAN TISSUE, FROM WHOLE BODIES TO JUST A FEW CELLS.

Asia has frozen mummies, too. About 2,500 years ago, nomads called the Pazyryk lived in the grassy, treeless plains of Siberia. Their dead leaders were buried in deep graves covered by mounds of soil. Inside, their bodies were protected by the region's severe cold. From one of these graves, or kurgans, came a woman now known as the Ice Maiden. Her

AN EGYPTIAN MUMMY, STILL INSIDE ITS COFFIN, ENTERS A BODY SCANNER. THE SCANNER EXAMINES THE INSIDES.

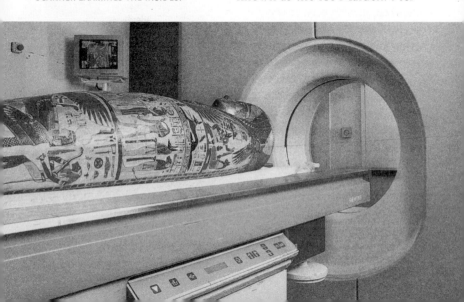

body was decorated with tattoos, and she had been buried in her finest clothes.

## Egyptian mummies

Among the world's mountain of mummies, it's the ones from ancient Egypt that were the most elaborately preserved. Skilled embalmers used knives and hooks, salts and perfumes, and packing and bandages to prepare a body for everlasting life. And not just human bodies either! If it had a heartbeat, the Egyptians mummified it. Cats, dogs, birds, fish, snakes, mice, and even beetles were mummified if they were needed as pets in the afterlife or if they represented certain gods.

At first, Egyptian mummies were made by accident. The earliest Egyptians buried their dead in pits dug into the land's hot, dry sand. The bodies dried out, and Egypt's first mummies were "born." But when we think of Egyptian mummies, it's the ones carefully wrapped in bandages that come to mind. These "true" mummies were made from at least 2600 BCE.

## Learning from mummies

Not so long ago, scientists used to unwrap and cut open mummies to find out about a person's age, health, diet, and what they died from. This is rarely done now. Today's scientists use technology such as X-rays, body scanners, radiocarbon dating, and DNA analysis to learn about people from the past. These methods of research are nondestructive, which means the mummies are left in good shape. That's important, because once a mummy was a real person—someone who hoped that when

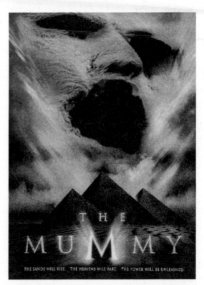

FROM THE EARLIEST DAYS OF SILENT BLACK-AND-WHITE CINEMA TO TODAY'S SPECIAL-EFFECTS BLOCKBUSTERS, MUMMIES HAVE BEEN MADE INTO MOVIE STARS.

they died, their body would be left in peace. Today's scientists respect the dead, which is why they do as little as possible to disturb a mummy's sleep.

# EGYPT—THE GIFT OF THE NILE

The civilization of ancient Egypt lasted for more than 3,000 years. It flourished along a thin strip of fertile land that lay on either side of the River Nile. For the people who lived there, this great river brought life and prosperity. Their land was "the gift of the Nile," and their magnificent culture became one of the greatest the world has ever known.

**Egypt's great highway**

The River Nile is the world's longest river, flowing north for about 4,145 miles (6,740 km) from its source in Burundi, East Africa, to the Mediterranean Sea. The civilization of ancient Egypt owed its very existence to this mighty, life-giving river. The Nile watered the land and crops grew in abundance along its banks. It was also easy to navigate and provided a highway between the upper and lower parts of the country. The river's floodplain was narrow, ranging between

THE EASIEST WAY TO TRAVEL IN EGYPT IS BY RIVER. THAT'S AS TRUE TODAY AS IT WAS FOR THE ANCIENT EGYPTIANS.

1 and 25 miles (2 and 40 km) wide, and it was along this thin green belt of land that the ancient Egyptians lived.

**The Nile in flood**

Every year, summer rains in the mountains at the source of the Nile caused the river to

THIS IS EGYPT SEEN FROM SPACE. YOU CAN SEE THE NILE WINDING ITS WAY TOWARD YOU FROM ITS SOURCE IN EAST AFRICA.

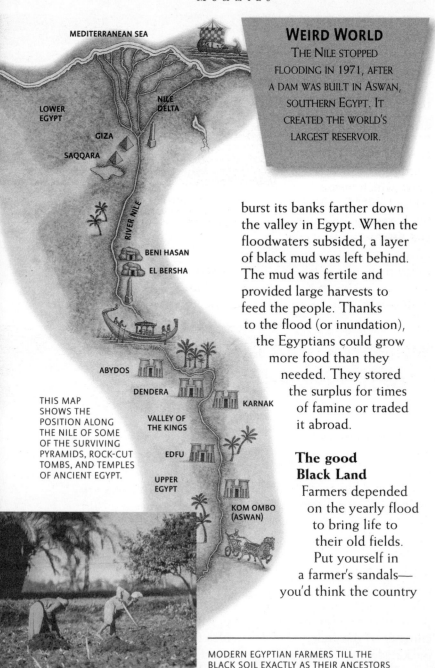

MEDITERRANEAN SEA

LOWER EGYPT

NILE DELTA

GIZA

SAQQARA

RIVER NILE

BENI HASAN

EL BERSHA

ABYDOS

DENDERA

KARNAK

VALLEY OF THE KINGS

EDFU

UPPER EGYPT

KOM OMBO (ASWAN)

THIS MAP SHOWS THE POSITION ALONG THE NILE OF SOME OF THE SURVIVING PYRAMIDS, ROCK-CUT TOMBS, AND TEMPLES OF ANCIENT EGYPT.

burst its banks farther down the valley in Egypt. When the floodwaters subsided, a layer of black mud was left behind. The mud was fertile and provided large harvests to feed the people. Thanks to the flood (or inundation), the Egyptians could grow more food than they needed. They stored the surplus for times of famine or traded it abroad.

## The good Black Land

Farmers depended on the yearly flood to bring life to their old fields. Put yourself in a farmer's sandals— you'd think the country

MODERN EGYPTIAN FARMERS TILL THE BLACK SOIL EXACTLY AS THEIR ANCESTORS DID IN THE TIME OF THE PHARAOHS.

had been born again because the squelchy black mud dumped by the Nile was new land. The Egyptians lived their lives around this yearly cycle and even named their country after the mud. Their word for Egypt was *Kemet*, which means "Black Land." To them, black was a good color, and *Kemet* was a land of plenty. No wonder they called themselves *remetch en Kemet*—"the people of the Black Land."

EGYPT WOULD NOT EXIST WITHOUT THE NILE. ITS BANKS ARE LUSH AND FERTILE, BUT BEYOND THIS LIE VAST SANDY DESERTS.

desert and death even clearer, the Sun set in the west. At dusk, it sank slowly from sight,

# WHEN THE NILE FLOODED, THE PEOPLE SAW THEIR LAND REBORN.

## The bad Red Land

Beyond the narrow fertile strip was a vast sandy desert. The ancient Egyptians called the desert *Deshret*, meaning "Red Land." To their way of thinking, the dry red sand of *Deshret* was a place of death—it was the complete opposite of *Kemet*.

What's more, the desert in the west was said to be the entrance to the underworld, the kingdom of the dead. As if to make the link between the

as if it were being extinguished and swallowed by the desert.

## A land of opposites

Ancient Egypt was a land of two very different parts— one part wet and fertile where nearly everyone lived, and one part dry and barren where almost no one lived. The ancient Egyptians were great believers in what we call "duality," the idea that everything has an exact opposite, like good and evil, living and dead. This idea

17

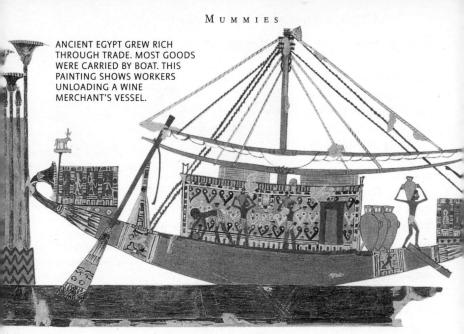

ANCIENT EGYPT GREW RICH THROUGH TRADE. MOST GOODS WERE CARRIED BY BOAT. THIS PAINTING SHOWS WORKERS UNLOADING A WINE MERCHANT'S VESSEL.

of opposites crops up time and again in the ancient Egyptian world.

## The opposite of Egypt

The ancient Egyptians believed that Egypt itself had a heavenly opposite in the afterlife. This was where all Egyptians longed to travel after death—to a perfect world where they would enjoy eternal life. Belief in the afterlife was so strong that the ancient Egyptians went to extraordinary lengths to prepare for it. The most important preparation was to preserve the dead body, especially the face, in a lifelike way. This was crucial if a dead person's spirit was to recognize its old body after death. If the spirit couldn't find its body

when it returned to the tomb, everlasting life would not begin. Preparations for the journey after death were also elaborate. Tombs were crammed with everything the Egyptians thought they might need in the afterlife—and they did not travel light!

## Our knowledge of Egypt

Many clues to Egypt's past have disappeared. Thieves have stolen treasures. Desert sands and time itself have worn away the ancient villages and cities.

THIS GIANT STATUE OF PHARAOH RAMESSES II (REIGNED 1279–1213 BCE) SHOWS HIM WEARING THE DUAL CROWN, REPRESENTING HIS RULE OVER THE TWO LANDS (NORTHERN AND SOUTHERN EGYPT).

But still we know a great deal about the ancient Egyptians. We can read their writing, study their stone monuments and everyday objects, and quite literally come face to face with the people themselves. Egypt's dry climate is ideal for preserving bodies. The oldest surviving mummies are about 4,000 years old. They "speak" to us about the world in which they lived— a world unbelievably distant and different from our own. But above all, mummies are amazing evidence of the ancient Egyptians' desire to survive death and live forever in the mysterious afterlife.

**WEIRD WORLD**

EGYPTIANS THOUGHT THAT, IN THE AFTERLIFE, THEY WOULD STILL NEED TO WORK IN THE FIELDS. THE RICH WERE BURIED WITH MODEL "SHABTI" FIGURES TO DO THE HARD WORK FOR THEM.

# EVERLASTING LIFE

The ancient Egyptians' idea of heaven was a garden paradise. They called it the Field of Reeds—a place where the sun shone and people worked happily harvesting crops. It was very similar to Egypt, except that the grain grew much taller and everything was perfect! But the journey to the afterlife was full of danger and passed through the underworld—an ordeal for which every Egyptian wanted to be prepared.

## The cycle of life

According to the ancient Egyptians, life was a series of changes. You entered this world as a baby. As time passed, the baby changed into a child and then into an adult. The final change came with death. The Egyptians didn't think

THIS MODEL IS OF A BOAT CARRYING A COFFIN TO ITS BURIAL PLACE.

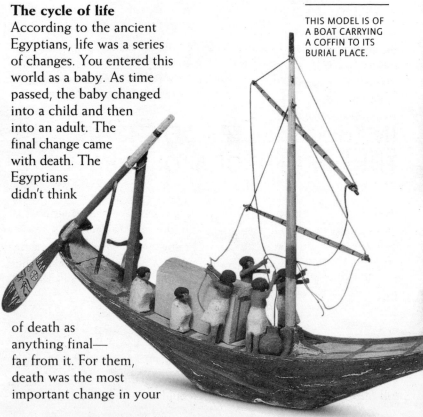

of death as anything final— far from it. For them, death was the most important change in your

A PERSON'S BA (SPIRIT FORM) WAS ALWAYS SHOWN AS A BIRD WITH A HUMAN HEAD.

cycle of life. It marked the point at which you began another existence in a better place. Their way of describing

snakes and lakes of fire. A simple coffin wasn't protection enough against dangers such as these, so the Egyptians made

# IN ANCIENT EGYPT, DEATH WAS THE FINAL LEG OF A JOURNEY.

death was "the night of going forth to life." But before you could reach the afterlife, there was a long and terrifying journey to make through the underworld and an examination of your past life.

### The Book of the Dead

Parts of the underworld were full of horrors, such as deadly

sure they were armed with hundreds of magic spells to help them through. These came from an ancient work called the Book of the Dead. Spells were written on the coffin or on a scroll tucked in with the mummy, together with a map of the underworld. The Book was your passport. If you could recite the correct spells, you would get through unharmed.

## The hall of Two Truths

The ultimate danger in the underworld was failing the test set for you in the hall of Two Truths. This was where your heart was weighed against a feather, the symbol of truth, to see if you deserved everlasting life. The jackal-headed god Anubis presented you before a jury of gods, who accused you of crimes committed during your life, which you denied. If your denial was true, the god of wisdom, Thoth, wrote that you were "true of voice" and let you through to the afterlife, where you lived forever. An awful punishment awaited if you were untruthful. Your heart was thrown to the crocodile-headed goddess Ammut, called "the devourer of the dead," who sat behind Thoth.

## The two spirits

The Egyptians believed that everyone possessed certain spirit forms, which were released from the body

THE MOST IMPORTANT MOMENT IN A MUMMY'S "LIFE" IS THIS CEREMONY BEFORE THE GOD ANUBIS. HERE, A DEAD MAN'S HEART IS WEIGHED AGAINST THE FEATHER OF TRUTH.

after death. The main ones were called the *ka* and the *ba*.

The *ka* was your "invisible twin" and your life force. While you were alive, the *ka* lived only inside your body. But at the moment of death, it was free to come and go as it wished. It still used the body as its home, and this is why preserving the body was so important. The *ka* also needed food and drink, which were provided through offerings or images of food placed in the tomb.

The *ba* was a spirit form which could move around, traveling between the tomb and the underworld. The *ba* could eat, speak, and even visit the land of the living. It was usually pictured as a bird with a human head. To live forever, your *ka* and *ba* had to be reunited in the tomb with your mummy. Once this happened, you would become immortal. But before you could hope for everlasting life, you had to spend this life being careful not to offend any of ancient Egypt's numerous gods.

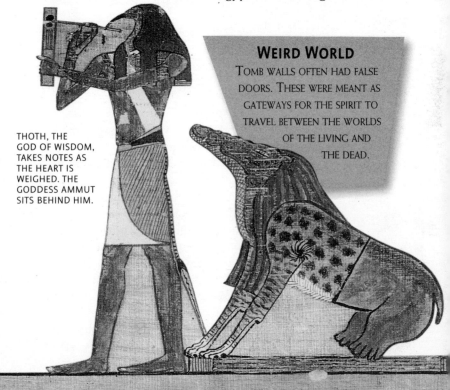

THOTH, THE GOD OF WISDOM, TAKES NOTES AS THE HEART IS WEIGHED. THE GODDESS AMMUT SITS BEHIND HIM.

## WEIRD WORLD

TOMB WALLS OFTEN HAD FALSE DOORS. THESE WERE MEANT AS GATEWAYS FOR THE SPIRIT TO TRAVEL BETWEEN THE WORLDS OF THE LIVING AND THE DEAD.

# ENTER THE GODS

The ancient Egyptians had a bewildering number of gods. There may even have been as many as 2,000. Many gods appear in several different forms, so it's often difficult to work out who's who. Over time, some gods grew in importance and others declined. In the end, of course, they all lost their power and died out as Egyptian religious beliefs changed. But the gods' mysterious natures, tall crowns, and animal heads continue to fascinate and haunt.

AMUN-RA WAS THE KING OF THE GODS. HE WORE A CROWN OF TALL FEATHERS.

**Local gods**

Most of ancient Egypt's gods were minor figures worshipped in only a few towns and villages. Deities that fit into this group are called local gods.

THE *WEDJAT* EYE WAS A COMMON AMULET. IT REPRESENTED THE EYE OF HORUS AND WAS WORN FOR PROTECTION.

Some minor gods, such as Bes, were popular with ordinary Egyptians. People kept pottery statuettes of Bes in their homes. These showed him as a little bearded man with his tongue sticking out. Bes was believed to protect households, watching over women giving birth and their children. He drove away snakes, scorpions, and evil spirits.

## Gods with creature heads

Many Egyptian gods were shown with human bodies and the heads of animals, birds, or was Re-Harakhty, the great hawk soaring in the sky. At night, when he traveled through the underworld, he had

# THE GODS HELD POWER IN EGYPT FOR MORE THAN 3,000 YEARS.

insects, depending on which one represented their power. Some had a variety of animal forms. For example, at dawn, the sun god was shown as Khepri, the scarab-beetle, rolling the sun disk above the eastern horizon. Later in the day, he the head of a ram. Thoth, the god of scribes and learning, was sometimes shown as a baboon and at other times as an ibis.

OSIRIS WAS THE GOD OF THE UNDERWORLD. HIS KINGDOM WAS THE GHOSTLY "OPPOSITE" OF EARTHLY EGYPT.

Other gods, such as Anubis
with a jackal's head or Osiris
with his green face, are easier
to recognize! Today, some of
these gods may appear bizarre
and even scary, but to the
Egyptians, they were like
familiar old friends.

**The gods of power**
The gods and goddesses
that mattered most were the
universal deities—dynamic
beings with fantastic powers
and important jobs to do.
They were the gods whose
statues and pictures were
everywhere and whom
people loved or feared.

Great temples were built
for these deities, who were
worshipped throughout the
land as part of the official, or
state, religion of Egypt. These
gods were the immortals who
brought order into the world.

Without them, the world
would be in total chaos,
so everyone thought.

**WEIRD WORLD**
EVER SEEN A FOSSIL
CALLED AN AMMONITE?
IT LOOKS LIKE THE CURLED-
UP HORN OF A RAM.
IT WAS NAMED AFTER
THE RAM-HEADED
GOD AMMON.

OSIRIS WAS SHOWN
WITH A GREEN FACE,
SYMBOLIZING EGYPT'S
PLANT LIFE AND REBIRTH.

## Ra and Amun

Ra (also called Re) was for a long time the most important god of all. He was the sun god—the god upon whom all life on Earth depended. He was the shining sun itself. Closely linked with Ra was Amun. At first, he was worshipped as a local god in Thebes, the ancient capital of Egypt. But as Thebes became more important, so, too, did Amun. In time, he became the creator god—the god who was said to have created all the other gods. As his powers changed, so did his name. Because of his links with Ra, his name became Amun-Ra.

ISIS, SHOWN HERE HOLDING HER SON HORUS, HAD GREATER MAGICAL POWER THAN THE OTHER GODS.

## Osiris and Isis

One of the most-loved gods was Osiris. He had triumphed over death, and every Egyptian wanted to follow his example. Osiris was the god of rebirth. He was also the ruler of the underworld.

Far back in history, Osiris was said to have been a good pharaoh who brought civilization to Egypt. When he took his sister Isis as his queen, he was killed by his jealous brother Seth, the god of chaos, storms, and war. Seth chopped Osiris's body into pieces and scattered them throughout Egypt. Isis collected the pieces and made them into the first mummy. Osiris was then reborn and lived on to rule the dead. He was the first king to survive death. Through believing in Osiris and the story of his rebirth, people hoped they, too, would have life after death.

## Horus

Isis's son by Osiris was Horus, the god of the sky. When Horus grew up, he avenged his father's murder by killing Seth and taking the throne of Egypt. But during the battle with Seth, he lost an eye. The Eye of Horus, or *Wedjat* Eye, became a symbol of victory over evil.

## Anubis

There's a doglike animal in Egypt that has a habit of prowling around cemeteries at night. It's the jackal, and because of its liking for the places where the ancient Egyptians buried their dead, it became associated with death itself. It was probably because of the jackal's taste for corpses that Anubis, a god with the head of a jackal, was made

# THE JACKAL WAS LINKED TO DEATH BECAUSE OF ITS TASTE FOR CORPSES.

BASTET, THE CAT GODDESS, WAS THE DAUGHTER OF RA. SHE WAS A PROTECTIVE MOTHER GODDESS.

the protector of the dead. But, unlike a real jackal, which has brown fur, Anubis was colored black. This was the color of the fertile mud left by the flooding of the River Nile. Mud represented the rebirth of the land, and mummification was the process of being reborn.

## The daddy of mummies

Anubis was the god of mummy making. It was his job to preserve a body for eternity. According to legend, the first body Anubis mummified was that of Osiris.

Every mummification was a magical act, meant to recreate the making of the very first mummy, of Osiris by Anubis. The role of Anubis was played by a priest, called the Overseer of Mysteries, wearing a mask of the god.

THE ANUBIS PRIEST OVERSEES THE MUMMIFICATION OF A TOMB BUILDER NAMED SENNEDJEM.

# WRAPPED FOR ETERNITY

**M**ummy making was perfected in a land that had plenty of the ingredients needed to preserve a body naturally—heat and sand. Egypt's hot, dry climate seemed to preserve buried corpses and even keep them looking lifelike. This made the ancient Egyptians wonder whether they could preserve bodies for the afterlife. Once they'd discovered how to stop a corpse from rotting, the mummy makers set about refining their amazing craft.

EVEN THE EARLIEST SAND MUMMIES WERE BURIED WITH GOODS FOR THE AFTERLIFE, LIKE JEWELRY.

### The mummy age

Throughout the vast era of ancient Egyptian history, one thing never changed. This was the powerful belief that a person would live forever in the afterlife if their body was somehow preserved. As the centuries passed, Egyptian mummy makers continually improved their embalming techniques in order to make everlasting life a reality.

As a result, mummies were made in Egypt for about 5,000 years. The

HOT, DRY DESERT SAND PRESERVED BURIED BODIES AND PREVENTED THEM FROM DECAYING.

oldest mummy yet found was made in 4600 BCE, and the last ones around 400 CE.

## The first Egyptian mummies

Long before the ancient Egyptians started to make mummies, nature was doing it for them. From around 5000 BCE, they buried their dead in shallow pits scooped into the desert sand. Bodies were placed lying on their sides in a sleeping position, along with simple offerings, such as shells, beads, and pots. The hot, dry sand preserved the bodies, leaving the skin hard and leathery.

Ancient Egyptians may have accidentally discovered that corpses of the dead survived burial and decided to find even better ways to preserve them. By 4600 BCE, they had begun to wrap the dead in linen bandages, coated with a thick varnish made from resin along

with aromatic plant extracts, which killed bacteria.

## New beliefs

Preserving the dead led to new ways of thinking about death. Egyptians began reasoning that if a dead person was to be reborn

### WEIRD WORLD
ALL OF THE ORGANS WERE SAVED EXCEPT FOR THE BRAIN, WHICH WAS THROWN AWAY. EGYPTIANS BELIEVED THAT THOUGHTS CAME FROM HEARTS, NOT BRAINS.

RICH MUMMIES WERE WRAPPED IN LINEN BANDAGES, WITH MAGICAL AMULETS FOR PROTECTION.

and live again, the person's body had to be preserved in the most lifelike way possible. It would become a "home" for the body's spirits (the *ka* and the *ba*).

Over time, methods of embalming the dead improved. Egyptians learned to remove the inner organs, which quickly rot, preserving them separately in jars. By the time of the era known as the New Kingdom (c.1550–1070 BCE), the embalmers had perfected their art.

AT THE FUNERAL, FAMILY MEMBERS BROUGHT OFFERINGS TO THE MUMMY IN HIS OR HER TOMB.

### Brain drain
They began by removing the brain. Long hooks made from bronze were pushed up through the nostrils and the hole at the base of the skull where it joins the spine. The hooks were then whisked around inside the skull until the brain was a soupy liquid that could be pulled and

# THE PROCESS OF WRAPPING A MUMMY TOOK ABOUT 15 DAYS.

### A bloody business
Embalmers worked in open-air tents, close to the River Nile. They chose these places because they needed plenty of water to wash and clean the dead bodies. They probably also wanted plenty of fresh air to blow away the bad smells rising from their trade! When a grieving family brought a dead "customer" to the embalmers, the body was laid out on a flat wooden or stone table. The family was told to come back in 70 days, and the embalmers got to work.

drained from the head through the nostrils. When the skull was empty, it was filled with a hot, gooey fluid made from tree resin, beeswax, and sweet-smelling plant oils. As it cooled, it set hard.

### Removing the insides
Next, the embalmers started on the person's tummy area. A deep cut was made on the left side of the abdomen through which the organs were removed. Out came the lungs, liver, stomach, and intestines.

Each was then wrapped in linen bandages and packed into separate pots known as canopic jars. The heart was left inside the body, because the Egyptians believed it controlled a person's intelligence and emotions.

**Preserving salt**
The body was now a gutless, brainless, empty shell and was ready to be dried out. After washing the abdomen and chest cavity clean, it was packed with a natural, salty substance called natron. This

RICH EGYPTIANS COULD AFFORD TO BE BURIED IN MULTIPLE COFFIN CASES DECORATED WITH GOLD.

was collected from the edges of lakes. Natron did the same job as the hot sand of the desert—it absorbed water and other liquids. It also stopped the spread of mold and fungi and acted as an antiseptic that killed destructive bacteria. After being packed with natron, the body was then completely covered in a big pile of it and left for 40 days.

When the natron had done its job, the body was dried out. It was a ghastly sight! The skin was dark and blotchy all over and the legs were thin, like matchsticks. It was time for the embalmers to use their expert cosmetic skills to give the body a lifelike appearance.

### The natural look

First, the abdomen and chest were packed with linen, sawdust, and even mud to give the body shape. Sweet-smelling oils were then rubbed into the skin to make it soft and supple. The nostrils, ears, and mouth were plugged with wads of

**WEIRD WORLD**
WHEN ALEXANDER THE GREAT DIED IN 323 BCE, HIS BODY WAS EMBALMED AND PLACED ON DISPLAY IN A GOLD COFFIN FOR ALL TO SEE.

linen. The eyeballs, which shrank during the drying-out process, were replaced with balls of linen. Then the eyelids were pulled down over the eyes to give them a sleeping appearance.

Usually, the cut in the abdomen was sealed with wax. However, if the person was very important, a thin sheet of gold might be placed over the ugly-looking gash.

Last of all, a layer of molten resin was poured over the body to harden it up and make it waterproof. All this made the body look natural again.

### Wrapping up

With the embalming process over, it was time to wrap the body in layers of bandages. Thin strips of linen were used,

THE EMBALMERS DID A SUPERB JOB ON RAMESSES II. THEY KEPT HIS BIG NOSE ITS SHAPE BY STUFFING IT WITH PEPPERCORNS!

Once the body was covered in linen, the mummy's family would not see any mistakes the embalmers might have made. There are examples of a head that snapped off, then was fixed to the neck with a stick, and a queen whose face was so well stuffed with pads of linen that her cheeks burst open!

## Coffin fit

About 70 days after a person's death, their mummy was fitted inside a wooden coffin. For greater protection, it was sometimes placed inside a "nest" of several coffins, each colorfully decorated with spells to ward off evil. For real heavy-duty protection, given to the wealthy, the coffins were sealed inside a massive stone container called a sarcophagus, which could weigh several tons.

THIS NATRON IS IN ITS ANCIENT LINEN WRAPPING. NATRON IS STILL USED TODAY IN GOODS SUCH AS BAKING SODA.

often torn from worn-out clothes and furnishings. The body was wrapped in layer after layer, covering it from head to toe. During the wrapping process, priests chanted prayers and spells. Magic charms, called amulets, and jewelry were placed between the layers of bandages. These were to protect the person from harm during the long and difficult journey into the afterlife.

THIS FEMALE MUMMY IS PROTECTED BY DOZENS OF AMULETS. MANY ARE STILL HIDDEN AMONG HER BANDAGES.

All this helped the dead person through the terrors of the underworld, a place full of poisonous snakes, executioners, and lakes of fire.

**The journey to the tomb**
After the coffin lid was closed, the priests invoked the gods'

coffin walked mourners and priests who sprinkled milk and wafted incense. Behind it came a second sled carrying the canopic jars, the embalming leftovers, and goods the dead person would need in the afterlife—everything from food and fans to wine and wigs.

## COFFINS PROTECTED THE MUMMY FROM THIEVES AND EVIL MAGIC.

powers to help the mummy make it safely into the kingdom of Osiris.

The coffin was placed on a wooden sled, and a boat carried it across the River Nile to the west bank, the place where the sun set and the dead lived. Oxen and men then dragged the sled to the tomb. Ahead of the

A procession of servants were also used to carry the goods to the tomb.

**Brought back to life**
Once inside the tomb, the coffin was stood upright and a solemn ritual called the Opening of the Mouth was performed by a priest. While incense burned, the priest touched the mummy's mouth so that it could speak and

THE INTESTINES, STOMACH, LIVER, AND LUNGS WERE PLACED IN SEPARATE CANOPIC JARS.

eat again. He touched the eyes so that they could see, the nose so that it could breathe, and the ears so that they could hear. By restoring these senses, the body was reborn into a whole new existence. Once this was done, the tomb was sealed.

## Mummies are worth it

To the ancient Egyptian mind, the long and elaborate process of mummification was well worth the effort. It was the best way to ensure a successful afterlife. The *ka* would now be able to recognize its well-preserved former body and nourish it, and the *ba* would treat it as its home as it traveled between the afterlife and the tomb.

Egyptians who couldn't afford embalming or even a coffin for

protection took their chances on the journey. But even they were buried with protective spells, as these were vital if a dead person was to have any hope of completing the trip.

## The meaning of mummy

Mummy comes from the Arabic word *mummiya*. It has nothing to do with the English word we use for mother! *Mummiya* means bitumen, a type of sticky black tar. Why such an odd name to describe a preserved body from ancient Egypt?

INCENSE BURNS AND MOURNERS WAIL AS PRIESTS PERFORM THE OPENING OF THE MOUTH CEREMONY.

It originated when the Arabs visited Egypt, long after the art of mummy making had died out. They found some of the last bodies to be embalmed in Egypt between about 500 BCE and 400 CE. This was a time when embalmers took less care over their work. In their hurry to prepare a corpse, they filled it with molten resin, which turned the body black all over.

This puzzled the Arabs, who wondered what could have been used to blacken a body. They could only think of one thing: *mummiya*, or bitumen. In time, the word came into the English language, where it was shortened to "mummy."

# PYRAMID POWER

The pyramids of Giza are the largest stone buildings on Earth. They are precision-built supertombs designed to house a king's mummy for eternity and send his soul straight to the stars. When they were new and covered in dazzling white limestone, it must have seemed as though the gods themselves had created them. In fact, the pyramids were built by the people of the Nile Valley 4,500 years ago. Although we've learned a lot about them, many riddles remain.

THE SPHINX STANDS GUARD OVER THE PYRAMIDS OF GIZA. IT HAS THE BODY OF A LION AND THE FACE OF A KING.

**Tomb story**

The pyramids are unbelievably old. Even during the time of later pharaohs such as Tutankhamun, the pyramids were already ancient monuments. The kings who built them had become long-forgotten historical figures. But despite the extreme age of the pyramids, the story of Egyptian tomb building began even before the Pyramid Age.

**Mastaba tombs**

A lot of big changes happened in Egypt in about 3100 BCE. Lower and Upper Egypt united to become one country, and the age of the pharaohs began. Before this time, the dead were usually buried in simple pits in the desert. But after 3100 BCE, purpose-built, underground tombs with rooms became the fashion. To mark the tomb, a neat mound of mud bricks was built at ground level, right over the burial chamber.

This type of tomb is called a *mastaba*, from an Arabic word meaning "bench," because its low, flat appearance resembled the benches found outside Egyptian houses. Members of the royal family, the nobility, and wealthy individuals were buried inside *mastaba* tombs, but your ordinary Egyptian still began the journey to the afterlife from a sandy hole in the desert.

**From mound to pyramid**
During the reign of King Djoser (2667–2648 BCE), one of Egypt's first pharaohs, something very important happened at Saqqara, a vast cemetery in the desert. The pharaoh's architect, Imhotep, built a large *mastaba* for his master—but not from mud

UNDERNEATH DJOSER'S STEP PYRAMID AT SAQQARA IS THE KING'S BURIAL CHAMBER AND A VAST NETWORK OF PASSAGES.

Granite Ball & Bronze Hook
found in the small channels
from Queen's Chamber in the
Great Pyramid.
Discovered of and
Wayman Dixon
in 1872.

A HOOK AND STONE POUNDER ARE TWO OF ONLY THREE OBJECTS EVER FOUND INSIDE THE GREAT PYRAMID, WHICH WAS ROBBED IN ANCIENT TIMES.

shape, it's known as the Step Pyramid—and you can still see it today.

**The Pyramid Age**
Djoser's Step Pyramid started a new fashion. For the next 800 years, the pharaohs ordered the building of pyramids throughout the land. They were tombs fit for Egypt's rulers.

At first, the pyramid builders made step pyramids, like Djoser's. Then, during the reign of the pharaoh Sneferu (2613–2589 BCE), someone had

bricks. Instead, he used stone. And Imhotep's inventiveness didn't stop there. On top of the king's *mastaba*, he added a smaller stone platform, then a smaller one on top of that, and another and another.

# THE PYRAMIDS OF GIZA HAD ALL BEEN BROKEN INTO BY 1000 BCE.

Eventually the mound of stone rose up in a series of six huge steps. Perhaps it was meant to be a stairway to heaven, which King Djoser would climb after his death to join Ra, the mighty sun god. Whatever it represented, this building was ancient Egypt's first pyramid. Because of its

the bright idea of building a smooth-sided or "true" pyramid. But the builders got their math wrong. Partway through building Sneferu's pyramid, they realized the sides were far too steep. Questions were asked and heads were scratched. They couldn't very well knock it down and start again, so they changed the angle of the slope, which gave it a strange shape.

Sneferu was none too pleased with his tomb, which became known as the Bent Pyramid, so he had a second one built nearby, known as the Red Pyramid. This time, the builders got it right. From then on, the craft of building smooth-sided pyramids reached new heights.

It was Sneferu's son, Khufu (reigned 2589–2566 BCE), who created the most famous pyramid of all, at Giza, close to present-day Cairo. Made from around 2.3 million blocks of stone, each weighing around 2.75 tons (2.5 tonnes), the Great Pyramid is the largest ever built, rising 481 ft (146 m) into the sky.

**Planning the Great Pyramid**

Before work began, Khufu's architects had to find the right place to build. They needed a large area of flat land strong enough to support the weight

ARCHAEOLOGISTS HAVE DISCOVERED THAT THE GREAT PYRAMID WAS BUILT BY ABOUT 15,000 WELL-FED FREE WORKERS, NOT BY SLAVES AS PREVIOUSLY THOUGHT.

of the massive building. They also needed building stone—lots of it. The flat limestone plateau at Giza was the perfect place. Next, they recruited thousands of laborers and organized them into teams at the building site. Some carved rock at the nearby quarries, while others worked on the pyramid itself. But how was such a building constructed without the use of trucks, drills, or cranes?

**Blood, sweat, and tears**

The millions of limestone blocks used in the Great Pyramid were cut using simple tools of stone, copper, and wood—the ancient Egyptians didn't have the advantage of iron tools at this time.

Blocks were moved from the quarries to the building site on wooden sleds pulled by teams of sweating, shouting workers. The blocks then had to be lifted into place. Each

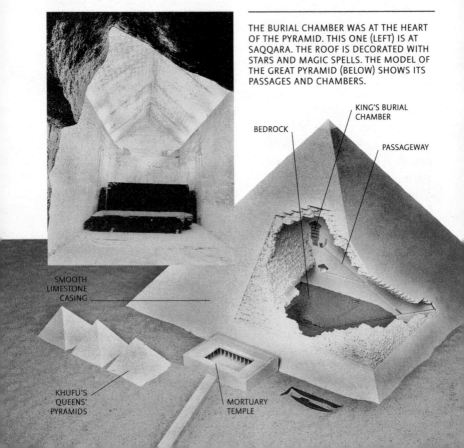

THE BURIAL CHAMBER WAS AT THE HEART OF THE PYRAMID. THIS ONE (LEFT) IS AT SAQQARA. THE ROOF IS DECORATED WITH STARS AND MAGIC SPELLS. THE MODEL OF THE GREAT PYRAMID (BELOW) SHOWS ITS PASSAGES AND CHAMBERS.

KING'S BURIAL CHAMBER

BEDROCK

PASSAGEWAY

SMOOTH LIMESTONE CASING

KHUFU'S QUEENS' PYRAMIDS

MORTUARY TEMPLE

chunk of stone weighed about the same as 40 adults, so it must have been a back-breaking job to haul them up the sides of the pyramid. How they did it is one of the mysteries of ancient Egypt.

There's little doubt that a sloping ramp made from crushed stone and sand was used, but no one seems to know what shape it was. It might have been a long, straight ramp; a ramp that zigzagged up one side; or even one that wrapped itself around all four sides of the pyramid.

## Finishing touches

When all the blocks were in place, the rough sides of the Great Pyramid were smoothed off with a layer of white, polished limestone. As this astonishing building neared completion, its tip may even have been crowned with a layer of gold.

All that was then needed was for the mummy of Khufu to be laid in his burial chamber, deep inside the pyramid.

## Pyramid precision

Even after 4,500 years, the Great Pyramid remains a masterpiece of geometrical design. Its four sides are aligned almost exactly with true north,

ONE OF THE SHAFTS IN KHUFU'S BURIAL CHAMBER POINTS TOWARD THE STAR CONSTELLATION OF ORION.

south, east, and west. No one is sure how such accuracy was achieved using only primitive tools. The pyramid contains a complex system of passages, chambers, and shafts. In fact, the two shafts found in the king's burial chamber point directly toward star constellations that were important to the ancient Egyptians—Orion and Sirius. The shafts were probably there to allow the king's soul to travel to the stars.

45

## The pyramid effect

The Great Pyramid had a dramatic effect on Egyptian civilization. Building it had been such a vast enterprise that the whole country was mobilized into supplying labor, food, and stone. The work had needed such organization, resources, and willpower that it transformed Egypt into an efficient and powerful state—in fact, the world's first true state. This was an awesome achievement.

## Pyramids perish

Fashions come and go, which is what happened with pyramids. As tombs, they were never ideal. Pyramids were often still unfinished when their kings died, and they were pretty obvious places to burgle. Pyramids were most popular among the rulers of the Old Kingdom (c.2686–2181 BCE). The ones built after this time were smaller and less well made, and by the time of the New Kingdom (c.1550–1070 BCE), a completely new type of tomb was in use for ancient Egypt's rulers.

THE PYRAMIDS OF GIZA WERE BUILT FOR THE PHARAOHS KHUFU, KHAFRE, AND MENKAURE. THE SMALLER PYRAMIDS WERE FOR THEIR CHILDREN AND QUEENS.

THE PYRAMIDS STILL INSPIRE ARCHITECTS TODAY, THOUGH NOW STEEL, CONCRETE, AND GLASS ARE USED. THIS ONE IS LOCATED OUTSIDE THE LOUVRE MUSUEM IN PARIS, FRANCE.

# TOMB RAIDERS

Ancient Egyptian royal tombs were difficult places to break into, with massive stone blocks sealing the entrances and false passages built to mislead robbers. But no burial place is truly safe—not if someone is really determined to raid the grave! In Egypt, pharaohs and ordinary folk both had the same worry— tomb raiders.

THIS GOLD MASK WAS FOUND IN 1922 IN TUTANKHAMUN'S TOMB, THE ONLY ROYAL BURIAL THAT HAD NOT BEEN ROBBED IN ANCIENT TIMES.

### WEIRD WORLD
ROBBERS FOUND THE TOMB OF QUEEN NEFERTARI, THE MAIN WIFE OF PHARAOH RAMESSES II, AND STOLE ALMOST EVERYTHING, INCLUDING THE MUMMY'S BANDAGES. ALL THAT'S NOW LEFT OF THE POOR QUEEN ARE HER KNEES!

**A grave business**
Tomb robbers were a tough bunch. First, they had to break into a tomb, which often meant tunneling through solid rock. They also needed strong stomachs, because robbing the dead could

48

ARCHAEOLOGIST HOWARD CARTER INSPECTS THE SECOND OF TUTANKHAMUN'S THREE COFFINS.

be a gruesome job. It wasn't only grave goods the robbers were after—statues, furniture, and the like. They also wanted the jewelry and amulets wrapped up in the mummy's bandages. It must have been like unwrapping a present, because the bandages concealed jewelry, precious amulets, and all kinds of small, portable treasures.

As tombs were filled with ever more valuable goods, tomb robbing increased. Robbers followed a simple rule: steal it, then sell it. Even though anyone caught in the act was tortured and put to death, the robbers weren't put off.

## Robbing the afterlife

To the ancient Egyptians, having their own tomb robbed was the ultimate nightmare. They really believed that a person's life in the next world would be ruined if someone broke into their tomb, opened their coffin, and, worst of all, destroyed the

ROBBERS ESPECIALLY WANTED SMALL ITEMS OF JEWELRY THAT WERE EASY TO HIDE AND SELL.

49

## WEIRD WORLD

IN 1881, THE BODIES OF MORE
THAN 40 ROYAL MUMMIES WERE
FOUND CRAMMED INTO ONE
TOMB. BECAUSE THEIR TOMBS
HAD BEEN DISTURBED
BY ROBBERS, A LATER
PHARAOH HAD COLLECTED
THEIR BODIES AND
REBURIED THEM.

tightly wrapped mummy in their haste to find treasure. Something had to be done. Most of all, the tombs of the pharaohs had to be protected.

## The secret valley

The pharaohs of the New Kingdom were the first to come up with a plan to defeat the robbers. From about 1500 BCE, they chose to be buried in a secret valley in the south of Egypt, far away from their traditional burial grounds at Saqqara and Giza. Today, this royal burial site is known as the Valley of the Kings. Over a period of about 500 years, some 60 pharaohs and nobles were buried there, in tombs cut into the rocky sides of the valley. Each tomb consisted of a sloping corridor with rooms leading off it. Some rooms were filled with grave goods, and one room contained the most precious item of all—the royal mummy, sealed inside a wooden coffin or a stone sarcophagus.

## The one that got away

The Valley of the Kings was supposed to be safe from thieving hands. Even though

THE WALLS OF TUTANKHAMUN'S BURIAL CHAMBER ARE DECORATED WITH SCENES SHOWING HIS FUNERAL AND HIS ARRIVAL IN THE AFTERLIFE.

the entrances to the royal tombs were hidden, the robbers—often the same people who'd dug the tombs in the first place—found them and looted them ... all except for one. By a stroke of luck, the resting place of a long-forgotten king was not robbed. His name was Tutankhamun, and when his tomb was found in 1922, it revealed wonderful things about the lives and riches of the pharaohs.

Archaeologists like Howard Carter, who made this famous discovery, are themselves modern-day tomb raiders. But unlike the robbers who risked death to sell stolen treasures, archaeologists send their finds to museums for people to study and marvel at the wonders of ancient Egypt.

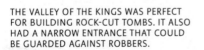

THE VALLEY OF THE KINGS WAS PERFECT FOR BUILDING ROCK-CUT TOMBS. IT ALSO HAD A NARROW ENTRANCE THAT COULD BE GUARDED AGAINST ROBBERS.

51

# THE PHARAOH — GOD-RULER OF EGYPT

For 3,000 years, ancient Egypt was ruled by kings and queens called pharaohs. From first to last, there were about 170 of them, and each one ruled with enormous power. Most pharaohs were men, but on rare occasions, Egypt was led by a woman. They were born as mortal people, but on the day the rulers were crowned, they were believed to be filled with divine power, and from then on the pharaohs were gods living on Earth.

THE PHARAOHS' JEWELRY WAS MADE IN ROYAL WORKSHOPS. THIS FINE GOLD CHEST ORNAMENT IS INLAID WITH GEMSTONES.

## The keeper of order

People believed the pharaoh was chosen to carry out the gods' work on Earth. The pharaoh was a god-ruler, filled with the spirit of the falcon-headed god Horus, and was responsible for the well-being of the world. At important religious festivals, pharaohs performed the temple rituals in person so the people could see them as a god-ruler. Ordinary Egyptians were in awe of their pharaohs. People were convinced

they had the power to keep the land of Egypt in good working order—and that meant everything from running the government to controlling the River Nile's floods. Of course,

STATUES OF PHARAOHS PORTRAY THEM AS POWERFUL, GODLIKE BEINGS. HERE, THE PHARAOH MENKAURE, WEARING THE TALL WHITE CROWN OF UPPER EGYPT, IS PROTECTED BY TWO GODDESSES.

52

A ROYAL FAMILY—AKHENATEN, HIS QUEEN NEFERTITI, AND THREE OF THEIR SIX DAUGHTERS. HE WAS A DARING KING WHO TRIED TO BANISH THE OLD GODS.

the pharaoh couldn't really control the yearly flooding of the Nile, but the ancient Egyptians didn't know that. So in years when the floods were low—people called these "bad Niles"—the pharaoh was blamed. A disaster, such as a poor harvest, reminded people how important the pharaoh's role was in daily life. In short, it was the god-ruler's duty to protect the world. If they didn't, people feared the world would plunge into chaos.

## The leader of the people

It's not easy for us to grasp what it meant to be a pharaoh, since we're dealing with ideas that seem alien to our modern way of thinking. However, the rest of the pharaoh's job description is quite straightforward.

The pharaoh was Egypt's head of state. As leader of the government, they controlled the army, the law, and the cults of all the gods. To help the pharaohs govern, they had thousands of priests, overseers, and officials who took care of Egypt's day-to-day administration. Among them were the viziers, or chief ministers. Viziers were the "chiefs of all the ruler's works" and were people with a lot of political power.

The pharaohs ruled their people from the royal palaces where they lived with family. Their ministers brought news about what was happening in the country, and important foreign visitors came to see them.

## Royal strength

If a pharaoh reigned for 30 years, a *sed* festival was held in their honor. This was a royal jubilee during which the pharaoh "died," was reborn, and then went through a second coronation ceremony. It was designed to renew the pharaoh's strength, giving them new power to carry on the

task of looking after Egypt. The highlight of the *sed* festival was when the pharaoh ran along a course to prove their fitness to rule.

## The royal regalia

Pharaohs had many items of regalia. They had crowns of different shapes and colors and a striped headcloth that came down over their shoulders. On their foreheads, the pharaohs wore a symbol of the cobra

### WEIRD WORLD
PHARAOHS WORE FALSE BEARDS TIED TO THEIR CHINS WITH CORDS. A BEARD WAS A SIGN OF A PHARAOH'S GODLIKE NATURE. EVEN WOMEN PHARAOHS WORE FALSE BEARDS!

RAMESSES THE GREAT RULED EGYPT FOR 67 YEARS. HIS LONG REIGN IS NOTED FOR ITS MANY GRAND BUILDINGS.

goddess Wadjet, whom people believed would spit flames at any enemies. The pharaohs held in their hands a crook-shaped scepter, which symbolized royal power, and a flail, which symbolized Egypt's fertility. The pharaoh even had a royal fly whisk for batting away flies!

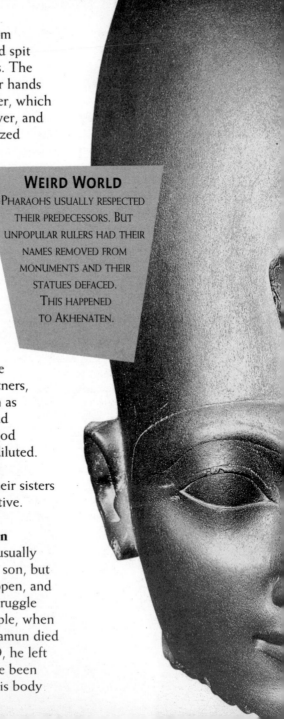

## WEIRD WORLD
PHARAOHS USUALLY RESPECTED THEIR PREDECESSORS. BUT UNPOPULAR RULERS HAD THEIR NAMES REMOVED FROM MONUMENTS AND THEIR STATUES DEFACED. THIS HAPPENED TO AKHENATEN.

## Choosing a spouse
As the ruler of Egypt was believed to be descended from the gods, it was difficult for a male ruler to choose his spouse. He could have many partners, but his queen (known as Great Royal Wife) had to be royal so the blood of the gods was not diluted. For this reason, kings sometimes married their sisters or a close female relative.

## The royal succession
The role of pharaoh usually passed from father to son, but this didn't always happen, and sometimes a power struggle took place. For example, when the pharaoh Tutankhamun died young, aged about 19, he left no sons. He may have been assassinated. While his body

was being embalmed, his elderly vizier called Ay took power as Egypt's next pharaoh.

The female pharaoh, Queen Hatshepsut, was another ruler who did not come to power in the usual way. When her husband Thutmose II died, her son was too young to become pharaoh, so she made herself the ruler of Egypt. Hatshepsut ruled wisely and after her death, her son Thutmose III took power. He removed his mother's name from her monuments, replacing it with his own.

## The god-ruler

The word pharaoh comes from the ancient Egyptian *per-aa,* or "great house," meaning the palace where the ruler lived. Over the years, the sense of the word changed, until by about 1350 BCE, it came to refer to the rulers themselves. The pharaoh had many titles, chief of which was Lord of the Two Lands—a reminder that Egypt had been formed by joining the lands of Upper and Lower Egypt. Another of their grand titles was Son of Ra. It meant the pharaoh was more than a ruler—they were a god.

THIS BUST MAY SHOW HATSHEPSUT OR HER SON THUTMOSE III, WHO RULED AFTER HER.

# TEMPLES — HOMES OF THE GODS

Ancient Egyptian temples were awesome structures. The grandest of them had giant statues, colorful walls, and vast halls lined with carved stone columns. Temples were central to the lives of the Egyptians, many of whom worked in temple farms and workshops.

### The purpose of temples

Ancient Egyptian temples were very different from today's churches, synagogues, and mosques. They were not meeting places for worshippers, but real, earthly homes for the gods. People believed the spirits of Egypt's gods actually lived and moved inside these sacred places.

Temples were also the centers for the religious cults that grew up around the gods. An important god would have a temple that might expand over time to become a huge complex containing offices, farms, schools, libraries, and

THE LOTUS FLOWER WAS A NATIONAL SYMBOL IN ANCIENT EGYPT. COLUMNS IN TEMPLES WERE OFTEN CARVED TO RESEMBLE LOTUS PETALS OR PAPYRUS LEAVES.

workshops. Temples were "living buildings" in every sense—they were continually enlarged and rebuilt, usually on the same spot.

### Step inside a temple

If you were an ordinary Egyptian, you wouldn't have been allowed very far inside a

THE TEMPLE OF DENDERA IS DEDICATED TO THE GODDESS HATHOR, WHOSE FACE GAZES OUT FROM ITS ENTRANCE.

## WEIRD WORLD

AT SOME TEMPLES,
WATER WAS POURED OVER
STATUES. PEOPLE THOUGHT
IT ABSORBED MAGICAL
POWERS AND COLLECTED
IT FOR USE AS MEDICINE.

STONE SPHINXES LINE
THE AVENUE LEADING UP
TO THE TEMPLE AT LUXOR.

temple. Your place was in the outer courtyards with the other lowly members of the public. Only priests and priestesses—the officials who lived and worked at the temple—could enter the heart of the building itself.

A large temple had a series of halls linked by a long corridor. As priests walked from hall to hall, they passed through "forests" of stone columns before reaching the temple's holiest place.

**The holy of holies**
The darkest, most holy room was located toward the far end of the temple, where the floor sloped upward and the ceilings became lower. A raised area inside the room symbolized the Egyptian creation story, in which the world was born as a sacred hill, rising from the ocean that surrounded it. Priests approaching this room may have imagined they were

clean clothes, and adorned it with jewelry. They then left gifts of food and sweet-smelling incense. This was to make the statue attractive to the gods so that they would live inside it. The priests believed these actions would protect the pharaoh, the people, and the world the Egyptians knew.

## Sacrifices to the god

Animals were sacrificed as gifts to the god. The Greek historian Herodotus described a sacrifice he had seen where wine was poured over a cow as an offering to the god. Then a priest slit the animal's throat and removed its head, which was sold in the market or thrown into the Nile. The carcass was stuffed with bread, honey, figs, and spices. Finally, the sacrifice was coated in oil and roasted while the priests chanted prayers. Once the god had "eaten" the meat, the priests would finish it. The smells of roasting sacrifices, incense, and smoke from torches must have given the temple a heady atmosphere.

on a journey to the hill of creation itself. It was a deeply mystical experience for them.

## Respect for the god

Inside the temple's holiest room was a statue of the god of the temple. Three times a day—at dawn, midday, and evening— the high priest washed the statue, anointed it with oil, dressed it in

THIS IS A PRIEST NAMED SEMATAWY. HE IS HOLDING A STATUE OF THE GOD ATUM.

# MAGIC SPELLS AND MEDICINE

The main gods of ancient Egypt played little part in everyday life, so ordinary people turned to magic to solve common problems. Their magic had nothing to do with making things appear and disappear. For the Egyptians, it was a form of medicine, just like a doctor's potions and powders. In fact, magic and medicine were linked very closely together.

THE ANKH WAS A POPULAR MAGIC CHARM.

**CILANTRO**

**CUMIN SEEDS**

**CASTOR OIL**

THE EGYPTIANS HAD A WIDE KNOWLEDGE OF HERBS AND THEIR MEDICINAL REMEDIES.

## Good spells, bad spells

Ancient Egyptians were convinced magic worked and conjured it up by the use of spells. People relied on magic to cure or ward off every type of day-to-day worry, such as disease, injury, and the risks of giving birth. They wore magic charms, or amulets, to heal themselves and keep danger away. They used spells to pass messages to ghosts, if a dead relative was upset or causing trouble.

Spells were also used to cause harm. These were curses. A person might write their enemy's name on a pot

> **WEIRD WORLD**
> HEADLICE WERE TREATED WITH CASTOR OIL AND OX FAT. THIS STOPPED LICE FROM BREEDING AND SUFFOCATED THEM!

A YOUNG NOBLEMAN IS PURIFIED WITH LIFE-GIVING WATERS AND SURROUNDED BY ANKH AMULETS.

SCARAB AMULETS WERE PLACED OVER A DEAD PERSON'S HEART TO HELP THEM THROUGH THE WEIGHING OF THE HEART CEREMONY.

or make a clay figure of them. Then, by smashing the object while uttering the spell, they hoped something nasty would befall the enemy.

## Powerful plants

The Egyptians had a detailed knowledge of healing plants, which they used hand in hand with magic. Today, science has shown us that many Egyptian remedies were genuinely effective. Garlic was very popular— it was used to prevent colds and the flu. Cilantro aided digestion, cumin eased the pain of arthritis, and castor oil was taken as a laxative.

## The magic of death

Coffins and mummies' bandages are full of evidence of the Egyptians' magic beliefs. Most rich Egyptians were buried with a copy of the Book of the Dead. This was a type of

magical route map to the afterlife, filled with spells to protect a dead person on the long journey. Some of the most powerful spells were written on amulets. For example, amulets known as heart scarabs were inscribed with a spell to stop a dead person's heart speaking out against them during the Weighing of the Heart ceremony (see pp.22–23). An outspoken heart might condemn its owner and ruin the chance of an afterlife. Placing heart scarabs between a mummy's bandages was thought to prevent this nightmare.

**WEIRD WORLD**
HEADACHES AND PRESSURE ON THE BRAIN WERE RELIEVED BY TREPANNING— CUTTING A HOLE THROUGH THE SKULL TO EXPOSE THE GRAY MATTER ITSELF!

## Doctors and knowledge

Doctors were important people in ancient Egypt, and they practiced magic and medicine in equal measure. Doctors knew a lot about the body and had some good ideas about what made it ill. They believed that people were born healthy and would not fall ill or die unless influenced by a harmful force. Science and magic came together to defeat this force through a mixture of medicines and spells.

Although there were no microscopes to see viruses and bacteria, doctors guessed that diseases came from wormlike creatures invading the body. They also understood that the heart "speaks out" through the head and hands—a reference to the pulse. In spite of this advanced knowledge, they believed the heart, not the brain, controlled intelligence and emotions. That's why embalmers preserved the heart and threw the brain away!

## Medicine and healing

The Egyptians wrote down much of their medical wisdom on scrolls. One such scroll contains 877 different ways to treat various illnesses and disorders, some of which are still used. Raw meat was applied to cuts (it prevents bleeding) and dressings were made from moldy bread (it stops the spread of harmful bacteria). Wounds were sewn up with needles and thread. Often, doctors only expected remedies such as these to relieve pain. Magic would provide the real cure.

A BRONZE SITULA (A TYPE OF BUCKET) WAS USED FOR SPRINKLING HOLY WATER— THOUGHT TO HAVE POWERFUL HEALING PROPERTIES.

# EVERYDAY LIFE

**M**ost people in ancient Egypt led busy lives. There was plenty of work to do in fields, quarries, and workshops throughout the land. The working day lasted for up to 12 hours, from dawn till dusk. But people didn't work all the time—they had fun playing games and socializing. At religious festivals and public celebrations, entertainers danced and made music. Everyday life was a mixture of work and pleasure.

## Happy New Year!

The Egyptian year began in mid-June, when the River Nile began to flood. As this event gave a new life to the land, it was a good time to say a new year had begun. There were 12 months in the year, which was divided into three seasons—flood, spring, and harvest. Each season had 4 months, and there were 3 weeks in each month. A week had 10 days in it, which meant each month had 30 days.

VILLAGES IN EGYPT TODAY HAVE CHANGED LITTLE SINCE ANCIENT TIMES. THEY STAND NEXT TO THE NILE, AND BUILDINGS ARE STILL MADE FROM MUD BRICKS.

## Planting the fields

In October, after the floodwaters had subsided, it was time for the farming year to begin. Farmers marked out their small fields in the fresh mud left by the river, then scattered emmer (a kind of wheat) and barley seeds. Farm animals were let into the fields to trample the seeds into the soil, burying them out of sight of hungry birds. Everyone in the family, young and old, was expected to help the animals and get stamping, too. The emmer wheat crop was Egypt's staple food, and

THIS MODEL SHOWS A MAN'S CATTLE BEING COUNTED TO FIND OUT HOW RICH HE IS.

67

it had to be tended and nurtured until it was time to harvest it in April and May.

## Animals on the farm

The most important farm animal was the cow. It was not only a source of meat and milk, officials counted everyone's cattle—the more a person had, the more tax they had to pay. Sheep and goats were raised for their milk, meat, wool, and hides. Their skins, when sewn up, were used to transport water. Poultry—geese, ducks,

# HUNTING LIONS IN THE DESERT WAS A FAVORITE SPORT OF PHARAOHS.

it was also used for work on the farm. The number of cattle a person owned was a measure of their wealth. At the start of each new year, government and hens—were kept for their eggs. Pigs were also kept, but people thought they were unclean. If you were a pig farmer, you were looked down upon by everyone! Donkeys

carried heavy loads, such as grain baskets. At harvest time, they trampled on the grain to remove the husks.

## Fruits and vegetables

Farmers were the most important workers in Egypt, producing vast amounts of food to feed the large population. Their fields looked like small square plots, a bit like the allotments we see around towns today. Apart from cereals, they grew onions, leeks, garlic, peas, lentils, beans, radishes, cabbages, cucumbers, and lettuces. Many fruits were grown, too, such as red grapes, figs, dates, and pomegranates.

FARMERS GREW MANY DIFFERENT TYPES OF FRUITS, VEGETABLES, CEREALS, AND HERBS IN THEIR FIELDS ALONG THE RIVER NILE.

## Food and drink

What would you have eaten in the days of the pharaohs? That depended on your place in society. The poor made do with bread, a few vegetables (mainly onions), fruits, and beer. This was the basic diet for adults and children. Beer, made from barley, was a thick, soupy liquid. It was nutritious and not very alcoholic. It was also safer to drink than Nile water, since this might be infected with parasitic worms and other bugs—but no one realized that at the time. As for meat, the Egyptians trapped hares, fish, and

AFTER PICKING THE GRAPES, WORKERS CRUSHED THEM BY TREADING. THE JUICE WAS THEN COLLECTED IN CLAY JARS.

wildfowl. Meat from oxen and wine were two luxuries that only the rich enjoyed with their daily meals. One thing eaten by both rich and poor was sand, which got blown into bread dough. Sometimes it was even added to grain to make it easier to grind!

The worn teeth of mummies are the tell-tale signs that the Egyptians chewed gritty bread.

## Houses made from mud

Architecture in ancient Egypt came in two different varieties. Grand buildings of stone, such as pyramids and temples, were

at one extreme, and people's homes, made from sun-dried mud bricks, were at the other. Even royal palaces were built using mud bricks. Stone buildings were built to last, as they were meant for eternity, but people's houses were made from the same mud that farmers used to grow their crops. If the River Nile flood was very high, it would wash away people's homes, recycling the bricks back into mud. Did the people mind? Perhaps they accepted it as part of life and set about rebuilding their homes with

new bricks. Houses were small and often joined together in groups that shared walls. Inside were one or two living rooms and a kitchen with a hearth. Most were single-story buildings, but in towns, houses might be two or three stories high. Roofs never changed— they were always flat.

## Games and toys

Life wasn't all work and no play. The ancient Egyptians found time to let their hair down. They liked to play board games, especially one called *senet*, which means "passing." The lucky winner made it through the underworld to the afterlife, but the loser didn't. Other games were more like sporting events, such as wrestling matches and stick fighting, played at religious festivals. Children played with balls and spinning tops, as well as models of people and animals.

## Song and dance

Music and dancing were important in religious and temple life, and also in nonreligious celebrations such as banquets. Musicians and

A COUPLE PLAYING *SENET* MOVE PIECES AROUND A BOARD OF SQUARES. THE ROUTE THE PIECES TOOK SYMBOLIZED THE JOURNEY TO THE AFTERLIFE.

dancers were both male and female. They blew flutes and other pipes; plucked the strings of harps; and shook bells, cymbals, and rattles. Women dancers were more in number, and sometimes they performed in pairs. They did

Most clothes were made from linen, a cloth woven from the fibers of the flax plant. Wool was rarely used. Egyptian clothes were simple—a loincloth or kilt for men and a close-fitting dress or loose wrap for women. Clothes were

# PAINTINGS IN TOMBS SHOW THAT EGYPTIANS LOVED A GOOD PARTY!

cartwheels, handstands, and backbends, and they learned their energetic dance routines by heart.

### Clothes and hairstyles

Just as our taste in clothes and hairstyles changes, so it did for the ancient Egyptians—though fashions came and went much more slowly than they do now!

usually left white, but some were dyed with plant and mineral extracts to decorate them red, blue, and yellow.

On their feet, people wore sandals made from palm leaves and rushes. Leather sandals were comfortable and lasted longer but were expensive.

Egyptian heads were adorned with wigs made from real human

FARM WORKERS CUT OFF THE EARS OF WHEAT AND BARLEY WITH COPPER SICKLES, THEN CARRIED THEM FROM THE FIELDS IN BIG BASKETS.

hair. A good wig was a status symbol rather like the "right" pair of shoes is today. Wigs were shown off at public events.

Children, especially boys, had their heads shaved except for a side patch, where their hair was left long. This was the "sidelock of youth," and it showed that the child was not yet thought of as an adult.

## Jewelry

Ancient Egypt was a nation of craftspeople, as well as farmers. Craft workers of extraordinary skill carved stone for statues, pressed clay to make pots, and worked with metals and semiprecious stones to create jewelry. Gold was the most valued of all metals used in making jewelry. Because it did not tarnish, gold was said to be a divine metal—the very

CROCODILES MADE THE NILE AND ITS BANKS DANGEROUS FOR EVERYONE, BUT CROCS WERE CONSIDERED SACRED ANIMALS.

flesh of Ra, the sun god. The connection with the gods made it the ideal metal to use in funerals. Tombs were filled with golden objects, and pharaohs like Tutankhamun had masks of solid gold.

Lesser people had masks of cartonnage (linen and papyrus stiffened with plaster). Some were covered in a wafer-thin layer of gold.

Beads and amulets were made from stones such as green feldspar, red jasper, and dark blue lapis lazuli—a stone that came from the region that is now Afghanistan. Lapis was rare and expensive, and a cheaper substance, called faience, was often used instead. Faience was a blue or green paste that could be shaped and fired like pottery.

THIS NECKLACE HAS AMULETS IN THE SHAPE OF COWRIE SHELLS, FALSE BEARDS, AND FISH. IN THE CENTER IS HEH, THE GOD OF INFINITY.

## An Egyptian family

Egyptians married young, with boys in their late teens marrying girls in their early teens. Some Egyptians waited until they were a bit older—but not that much older, since people weren't expected to live to

THESE COURTIERS APPEAR TO HAVE CONES TIED TO THEIR HEADS. THE CONE MAY HAVE BEEN A SYMBOL TO INDICATE THAT A PERSON WAS NICELY PERFUMED.

BRACELETS WERE WORN AROUND THE WRISTS, LIKE THIS ONE MADE FROM GOLD AND LAPIS LAZULI.

## No school!

The only schools in ancient Egypt were run by temples, and these were usually only for boys from wealthy homes. Very few children ever went to school. The government didn't do much to educate the people. After all, if boys were taught to be farmers, brick makers, carpenters, jewelers, or tomb builders (and tomb robbers) by their fathers, that was all the education they needed.

a ripe old age. Most were lucky if they made it to their forties. The purpose of marriage was to produce children.

As for girls, their mothers taught them all they

Parents wanted children since it was the duty of offspring to look after their mother and father as they grew old. Families often had as many as 10 children, and it was the mother's job to bring them up. However, when boys were old enough, their fathers took over, training them to be their assistants at whatever work they did.

needed to know about looking after a family and home.

The few privileged boys were given lessons in reading, writing, mathematics, and astronomy. Because they were literate—they knew how to read and write—they had a high status in society. These boys became the next generation of priests, scribes (clerks), and governors— the people needed to run the country.

# IMAGES IN WRITING

In July 1799, French soldiers found a remarkable object buried in the sand near the Egyptian village of Rashid, whose old name was Rosetta. The large slab of black stone they uncovered was the key to unlocking one of the world's greatest riddles—how to read hieroglyphs, the writing of ancient Egypt. Until this discovery, hieroglyphs had been a mystery for 1,400 years.

SCRIBES CHOSE THEIR SCRIPT IMAGES FROM THE WORLD AROUND THEM. THE OWL REPRESENTS THE LETTER "M."

## Cracking the code

For years, people had tried and failed to read hieroglyphs. But when the Rosetta Stone was unearthed, Thomas Young (1773–1829), an Englishman who could read 14 languages by the age of 12, realized it could help decipher the Egyptians' long-forgotten writing. The stone was carved with an identical inscription in two different languages—Egyptian (using two different scripts, or writing styles) and Greek.

Young compared the Greek with the Egyptian and slowly began to decode the strange signs and symbols. He hoped to be the first person to make sense of Egyptian writing. Eventually, it was a

### WEIRD WORLD

HIEROGLYPHS COULD BE WRITTEN FROM RIGHT TO LEFT OR LEFT TO RIGHT. YOU CAN WORK OUT THEIR DIRECTION BECAUSE THE HUMAN AND ANIMAL FIGURES ALWAYS FACE TOWARD THE BEGINNING OF THE LINE.

THE ROSETTA STONE IS AN ELABORATE LETTER OF THANKS WRITTEN TO PHARAOH PTOLEMY V IN 196 BCE.

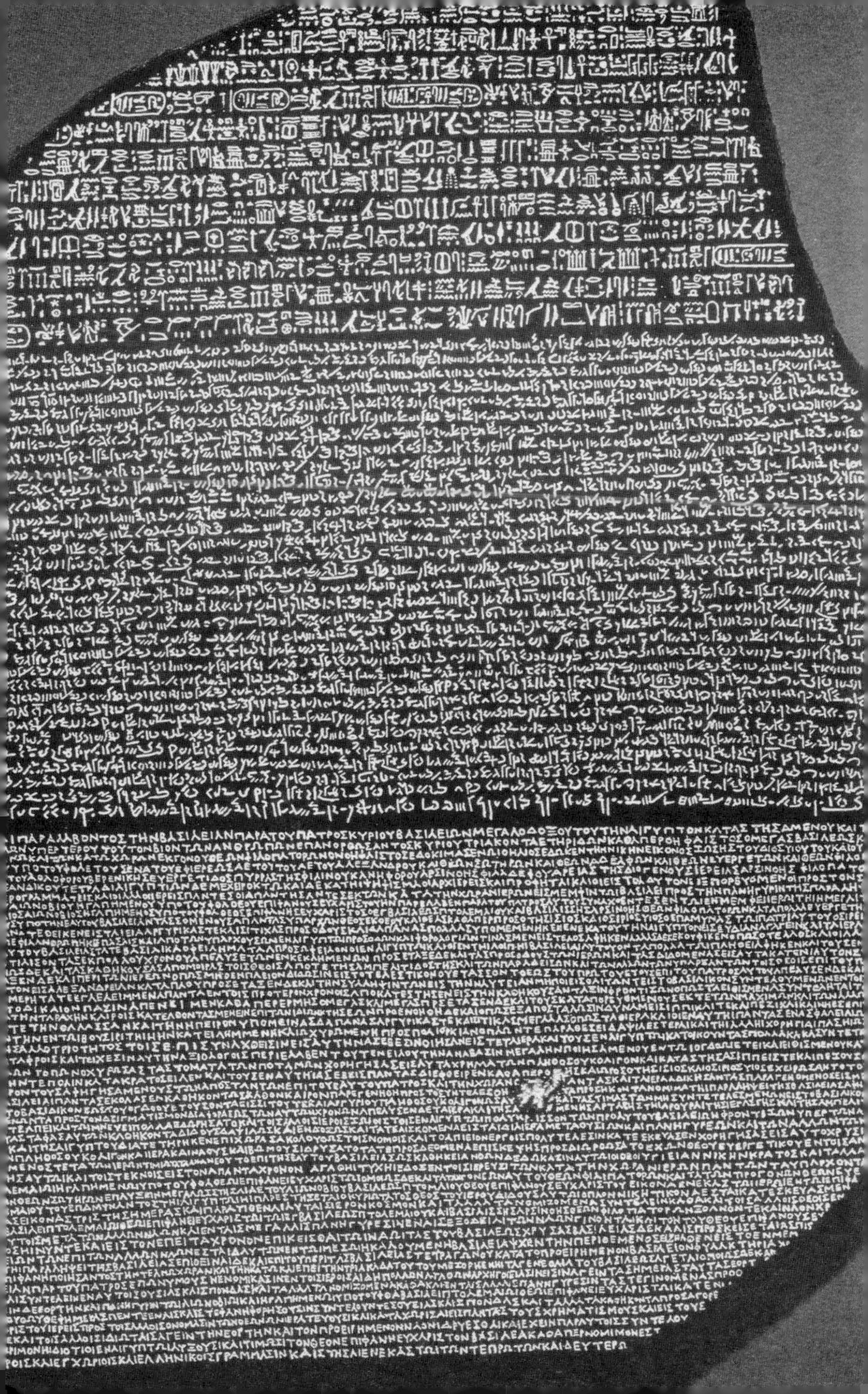

Frenchman, Jean-François Champollion (1790–1832), who made the real breakthrough. By matching royal names in the Greek and Egyptian scripts, Champollion used his knowledge of Greek to work out what hieroglyphs stood for. In 1822, he finally solved the puzzle.

SOME HIEROGLYPHIC SIGNS NEEDED A LOT OF PRACTICE BY SCRIBES AND ARTISTS ALIKE. HERE, AN ARTIST GOT CARRIED AWAY DRAWING A DUCKLING.

## Hieroglyphic confusion

The hieroglyphic script came into use about 3400 BCE. It was a system of writing in signs, which represented a mixture of sounds (as the letters of many modern alphabets do) and whole words. Other signs were used to clarify the meaning of a word so it wouldn't be misread. For most of ancient Egyptian history, there were about 700 hieroglyphic signs.

Hieroglyphs could be read from left to right or from right to left. They could be written in rows or in columns. If this sounds confusing, it was!

Because the writing system was so complex, only a small number of upper-class Egyptians learned to read and write. This helped the scribes keep their high status in society. Most people in ancient Egypt couldn't read or write.

Later, the ancient Greeks called it *hieroglyphikos*, meaning "holy signs," from which we get the word hieroglyphs. Because hieroglyphs were sacred, their most important use was for religious purposes. They were painted on coffins and carved in stone on the walls of temples and tombs. Hieroglyphs were also used for keeping economic records of harvests.

### Holy hieroglyphs

In ancient Egypt, writing, like so many other things, was thought to be of divine origin. It was the gift of Thoth, the god of writing and knowledge. The Egyptians called their writing *medu-netjer*, which means "the god's words."

A SCRIBE OFTEN HAD TO TRAVEL ON OFFICIAL BUSINESS, TAKING A WATER POT, REED PENS, AND INK IN A FITTED WOODEN CASE, LIKE THIS ONE.

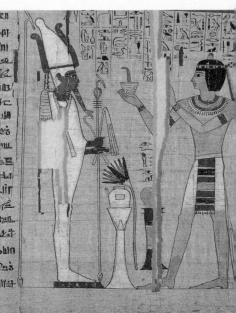

ON PAPYRUS, SCRIBES NORMALLY USED THE FAST FORM OF WRITING, HIERATIC. HERE, HIEROGLYPHS HAVE ALSO BEEN USED ABOVE A SACRED IMAGE OF OSIRIS.

## Rapid writing

Hieroglyphs represented the most formal way to write, but they weren't ideal. The signs were tricky and slow to draw. Busy scribes needed an easier, faster script for everyday use and developed one called hieratic, from a Greek word meaning "priestly." Hieratic was a shorthand for hieroglyphs and became the main script for business and private records.

By about 600 BCE, an even simpler script came into use. This one was called demotic, from a Greek word meaning "popular." Popular it might have been, but it's still thought that only 1 in every 100 people could read and write! Demotic is descended from hieroglyphs, but it's almost impossible to see any resemblance. The Rosetta Stone's message was written in demotic, as well as Greek and hieroglyphs.

THE PAPYRUS REED GREW ALONG THE NILE. IT WAS USED TO MAKE WRITING PAPER, ROPE, AND BOATS.

## Scribes

Scribes were those trained to read and write. They inherited their jobs from a parent and learned their craft by copying out texts over and over again. Their education started at age 9 and lasted for about 5 years. Scribes had to study hard and were beaten if they were lazy.

cut into strips, placed in two layers, then pounded together to form a strong sheet.

Before they got scribbling, a scribe sprinkled a few drops of water as an offering to the god Thoth. Taking up their reed pen, they dipped it into their water pot, then rubbed it over a block of dried ink—soot for black,

# THE MOST FAMOUS OF ALL SCRIBES, IMHOTEP, WAS MADE INTO A GOD.

But their years of training were worth the effort. Scribes were privileged and did not have to pay tax.

## Writing, paper, and ink

When they wrote, a scribe sat cross-legged on the ground. They pulled their kilt tight against the knees, making a flat surface on which to work. They wrote on paper made from the stems of the papyrus reed. The soft pith of the reed was

ocher (a mineral) for red—and began to write, brushing the ink onto their papyrus scroll. Both hieratic and demotic scripts were written from right to left. Because the ink took time to dry, a right-handed scribe had to be very careful not to smudge their writing as they worked across the scroll.

Scribes were trained professionals, and their work was usually neat and easy to read. It's from their words and records, as much as from mummies and tombs, that we know so much about life in ancient Egypt.

IMHOTEP WAS A TALENTED SCRIBE WHO ALSO DESIGNED THE FIRST PYRAMID, AT SAQQARA.

# ANIMAL MUMMIES

The ancient Egyptians mummified animals, sometimes with the same care they took when preserving people. Cats, dogs, cows, and fish were embalmed if they were associated with particular gods, or favorite pets, or simply needed for food in the afterlife. Toward the end of ancient Egyptian civilization, large cults grew up around certain animals, creating a massive demand for animal mummies for dedication to the gods.

CATS WERE SACRED TO THE GODDESS BASTET. FOR KILLING A CAT, THE PUNISHMENT COULD BE DEATH.

## WEIRD WORLD

IN THE 1800S, HUNDREDS OF TONS OF MUMMIFIED CATS WERE SHIPPED TO LIVERPOOL, ENGLAND, TO BE GROUND UP AND USED AS FERTILIZER ON FARMS!

THE EGYPTIANS WERE THE FIRST PEOPLE TO TAME AFRICAN WILD CATS AND KEEP THEM AS PETS.

## Afterlife menu

The Egyptians believed that dead people needed food in the next life, so supplies were buried with them. Joints of meat, whole birds, and fish were preserved, wrapped in bandages, and placed inside wooden coffinettes (little coffins) in the shape of the food. Some of these mummies were painted a brown color to make them appear roasted and ready to eat!

THIS GOLD CONTAINER HOLDS THE MUMMIFIED BODY OF AN IBIS. THESE BIRDS WERE DEDICATED IN THE MILLIONS TO THOTH, THE GOD OF SCRIBES AND WRITING.

## A pet is not just for life

Egyptians loved their pets and often wanted to take them to the afterlife. When their owners died, cats, dogs, gazelles, monkeys, and even ducks were buried in their owners' tombs. No one knows if a pet was killed and given the mummy treatment as soon as its master died, or whether it was allowed to live out its natural life.

## Animals with gods inside

Some animals were singled out for special treatment because people thought the spirits of the gods lived inside them.

This was particularly true of a sacred bull known as the Apis Bull, of which there was only ever one at a time. This animal was kept in luxury beside a temple, attended by servants and a harem of cows. When it died, it was embalmed with enormous care and ceremony. After removing its organs and placing them in giant canopic jars, the body was filled with

83

CROCODILES WERE SACRED TO THE GOD SOBEK. SOME TEMPLES KEPT TAME CROCS IN POOLS AND FED THEM MEAT AND WINE.

bags of sawdust and natron. It was then bandaged and buried with full honors.

**Animal mummy industry**
Toward the end of ancient Egyptian history, from about 300 BCE until about 400 CE, animals were mummified in vast quantities. Pilgrims could buy all kinds of creatures to give to the gods. Falcons, dogs, jackals, baboons, scorpions, snakes, crocodiles, and even scarab beetles were available as mummies. Some may have been "farmed" to provide a constant supply of bodies to the profitable mummy-making industry. An animal cemetery at Saqqara still contains an estimated 4 million ibis mummies, each in its individual burial jar. About 10,000 were buried there every year for around 400 years!

## WEIRD WORLD
A MUMMY ONCE THOUGHT TO BE A BIRD HAS TURNED OUT TO BE A HUMAN BABY, PROBABLY STILLBORN. IT HAD BEEN MUMMIFIED AS A FALCON.

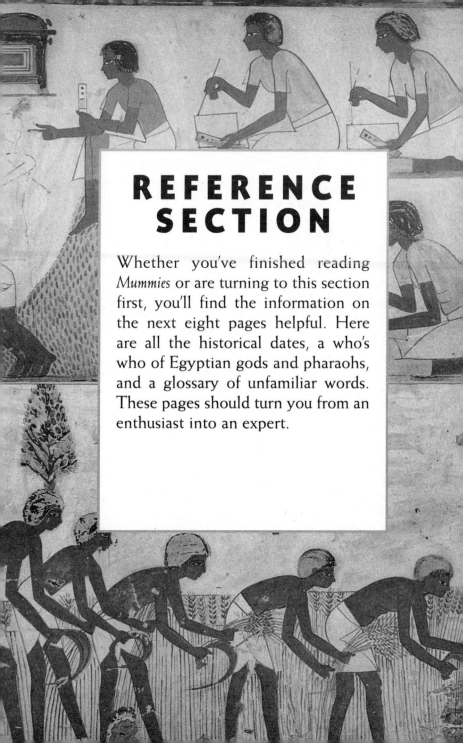

# REFERENCE SECTION

Whether you've finished reading *Mummies* or are turning to this section first, you'll find the information on the next eight pages helpful. Here are all the historical dates, a who's who of Egyptian gods and pharaohs, and a glossary of unfamiliar words. These pages should turn you from an enthusiast into an expert.

# ANCIENT EGYPT TIMELINE

Ancient Egyptian history is traditionally divided into three large parts, known as the Old, Middle, and New Kingdoms. There are also several smaller parts, known as periods. The 170 or so pharaohs who ruled ancient Egypt over the course of 3,000 years are ordered into 31 dynasties or groups. This simplified table lists the dynasties, their approximate dates, and year(s) when the pharaohs reigned.

## PREDYNASTIC PERIOD
5500–3100 BCE

## EARLY DYNASTIC PERIOD
3100–2686 BCE
**1st Dynasty** 3100–2890 BCE
Narmer (3100 BCE)
Aha (3100 BCE)
Djer (3000 BCE)
Djet (2980 BCE)
Den (2950 BCE)
Anendjib (2925 BCE)
Semerkhet (2900 BCE)
Qa'a (2890 BCE)

**2nd Dynasty** 2890–2686 BCE
Hetepsekhemwy (2890 BCE)
Raneb (2865 BCE)
Nynetjer
Weneg
Sened
Peribsen (2700 BCE)
Khasekhemwy (2686 BCE)

## OLD KINGDOM
2686–2181 BCE
**3rd Dynasty** 2686–2613 BCE
Sanakht (2686–2667 BCE)
Djoser (2667–2648 BCE)
Sekhemkhet (2648–2640 BCE)
Khaba (2640–2637 BCE)
Huni (2637–2613 BCE)
**4th Dynasty** 2613–2494 BCE
Sneferu (2613–2589 BCE)
Khufu (2589–2566 BCE)
Djedefre (2566–2558 BCE)
Khafre (2558–2532 BCE)
Menkaure (2532–2503 BCE)
Shepseskaf (2503–2498 BCE)
**5th Dynasty** 2494–2345 BCE
Userkaf (2494–2487 BCE)
Sahure (2487–2475 BCE)
Neferirkare (2475–2455 BCE)
Shepseskare (2455–2448 BCE)
Raneferef (2448–2445 BCE)
Nyuserre (2445–2421 BCE)
Menkauhor (2421–2414 BCE)
Djedkare (2414–2375 BCE)
Unas (2375–2345 BCE)
**6th Dynasty** 2345–2181 BCE
Teti (2345–2323 BCE)
Userkere (2323–2321 BCE)
Pepi I (2321–2287 BCE)
Merenre (2287–2278 BCE)
Pepi II (2278–2184 BCE)
Nitiqret (2184–2181 BCE)

## FIRST INTERMEDIATE PERIOD
2181–2055 BCE
**7–8th Dynasties** 2181–2125 BCE
Many minor pharaohs
**9–10th Dynasties** 2160–2025 BCE
Many minor pharaohs
**11th Dynasty** 2125–2055 BCE
Mentuhotep I

Intef I (2125–2112 BCE)
Intef II (2112–2063 BCE)
Intef III (2063–2055 BCE)

## MIDDLE KINGDOM
2055–1650 BCE
**11th Dynasty (continued)**
2055–1985 BCE
Mentuhotep II (2055–2004 BCE)
Mentuhotep III (2004–1992 BCE)
Mentuhotep IV (1992–1985 BCE)
**12th Dynasty** 1985–1795 BCE
Amenemhet I (1985–1955 BCE)
Senusret I (1965–1920 BCE)
Amenemhet II (1922–1878 BCE)
Senusret II (1880–1874 BCE)
Senusret III (1874–1855 BCE)
Amenemhet III (1855–1808 BCE)
Amenemhet IV (1808–1799 BCE)
Queen Sobeknerfu (1799–1795 BCE)
**13th Dynasty** 1795–1650 BCE
About 70 minor pharaohs

## SECOND INTERMEDIATE
**PERIOD** 1750–1550 BCE
**14th Dynasty** 1750–1650 BCE
Some minor pharaohs
**15th–16th Dynasties** 1650–1550 BCE
Sheshi
Khyan
Apepi I
Khamudi
**17th Dynasty** 1650–1550 BCE
Intef VII
Taa I
Taa II
Kamose (1555–1550 BCE)

## NEW KINGDOM
1550–1070 BCE
**18th Dynasty** 1550–1295 BCE
Ahmose I (1550–1525 BCE)
Amenhotep I (1525–1504 BCE)
Thutmose I (1504–1492 BCE)

Thutmose II (1492–1479 BCE)
Queen Hatshepsut (1479–1458 BCE)
Thutmose III (1458–1425 BCE)
Amenhotep II (1427–1400 BCE)
Thutmose IV (1400–1390 BCE)
Amenhotep III (1390–1352 BCE)
Amenhotep IV (Akhenaten)
(1352–1336 BCE)
Smenkhkare (1338–1336 BCE)
Tutankhamun (1336–1327 BCE)
Ay (1327–1323 BCE)
Horemheb (1323–1295 BCE)
**19th Dynasty** 1295–1186 BCE
Ramesses I (1295–1294 BCE)
Seti I (1294–1279 BCE)
Ramesses II (1279–1213 BCE)
Merneptah (1213–1203 BCE)
Amenmessu (1203–1200 BCE)
Seti II (1200–1194 BCE)
Siptah (1194–1188 BCE)
Queen Tausret (1188–1186 BCE)
**20th Dynasty** 1186–1069 BCE
Sethnakhte (1186–1184 BCE)
Ramesses III (1184–1153 BCE)
Ramesses IV (1153–1147 BCE)
Ramesses V (1147–1143 BCE)
Ramesses VI (1143–1136 BCE)
Ramesses VII (1136–1129 BCE)
Ramesses VIII (1129–1126 BCE)
Ramesses IX (1126–1108 BCE)
Ramesses X (1108–1099 BCE)
Ramesses XI (1099–1070 BCE)

## THIRD INTERMEDIATE
**PERIOD** 1069–747 BCE
**21st Dynasty** 1069–945 BCE
Smendes I (1069–1043 BCE)
Amenemnisu (1043–1039 BCE)
Psusennes I (1039–991 BCE)
Amenemope (993–984 BCE)
Osorkon the Elder (984–978 BCE)
Siamun (978–959 BCE)
Psusennes II (959–945 BCE)
*continued overleaf*

22nd Dynasty 945–715 BCE
Sheshonq I (945–924 BCE)
Osorkon I (924–889 BCE)
Sheshonq II (890 BCE)
Takelot I (889–874 BCE)
Osorkon II (874–850 BCE)
Takelot II (850–825 BCE)
Sheshonq III (825–773 BCE)
Pamai (773–767 BCE)
Sheshonq V (767–730 BCE)
Osorkon IV (730–715 BCE)
23rd Dynasty 818–715 BCE
Pedibastis I (818–793 BCE)
Sheshonq IV (780 BCE)
Osorkon III (777–749 BCE)
24th Dynasty 727–715 BCE
Bakenrenef (727–715 BCE)

## LATE DYNASTIC PERIOD
747–332 BCE
25th Dynasty 747–656 BCE
Piy (747–716 BCE)
Shabaka (716–702 BCE)
Shabitku (702–690 BCE)
Taharka (690–664 BCE)
Tanutamun (664–656 BCE)
26th Dynasty 664–525 BCE
Necho I (672–664 BCE)
Psammetic I (664–610 BCE)
Necho II (610–595 BCE)
Psammetic II (595–589 BCE)
Apries (589–570 BCE)
Ahmose II (570–526 BCE)
Psammetic III (526–525 BCE)
27th Dynasty 525–404 BCE
Cambyses (525–522 BCE)
Darius I (522–486 BCE)
Xerxes I (486–465 BCE)
Artaxerxes I (465–424 BCE)
Darius II (424–405 BCE)
Artaxerxes II (405–359 BCE)
28th Dynasty 404–399 BCE
Amyrtaeus (404–399 BCE)
29th Dynasty 399–380 BCE

Nefarites I (399–393 BCE)
Hakor (393–380 BCE)
Nefarites II (380 BCE)
30th Dynasty 380–343 BCE
Nectanebo I (380–362 BCE)
Teos (362–360 BCE)
Nectanebo II (360–343 BCE)
31st Dynasty 343–332 BCE
Artaxerxes III (343–338 BCE)
Arses (338–336 BCE)
Darius III (336–332 BCE)

## THE GRECO–ROMAN PERIOD 323–310 BCE
Alexander the Great (332–323 BCE)
Philip Arrhidaeus (323–317 BCE)
Alexander IV (317–310 BCE)

## PTOLEMAIC PERIOD 310–30 BCE
Ptolemy I Soter (305–285 BCE)
Ptolemy II Philadelphus
(285–246 BCE)
Ptolemy III Euergetes I
(246–221 BCE)
Ptolemy IV Philopator
(221–205 BCE)
Ptolemy V Epiphanes (205–180 BCE)
Ptolemy VI Philometor
(180–145 BCE)
Ptolemy VII Neos Philopator
(145 BCE)
Ptolemy VIII Euergetes II
(170–116 BCE)
Ptolemy IX Soter II (116–107 BCE)
Ptolemy X Alexander I (107–88 BCE)
Ptolemy IX Soter II (restored)
(88–80 BCE)
Ptolemy XI Alexander II (80 BCE)
Ptolemy XII Neos Dionysos
(80–51 BCE)
Ptolemy XIII (51–47 BCE)
Ptolemy XIV (47–44 BCE)
Queen Cleopatra VII (51–30 BCE)
Ptolemy XV Caesarion (44–30 BCE)

# FAMOUS PHARAOHS

## Narmer
REIGNED: 3100 BCE
FAMOUS FOR: being the first pharaoh
He united the kingdoms of Upper and Lower Egypt.

## Djoser
REIGNED: 2667–2648 BCE
FAMOUS FOR: the first pyramid
He built the Step Pyramid, at Saqqara.

## Khufu
REIGNED: 2589–2566 BCE
FAMOUS FOR: the Great Pyramid
Despite building the Great Pyramid at Giza, not a lot is known about Khufu. He must have been a powerful ruler, since the building of his pyramid would have involved mobilizing the whole country.

## Queen Hatshepsut
REIGNED: 1479–1458 BCE
FAMOUS FOR: peace and trade
Hatshepsut took power as Egypt's regent to look after the throne until Thutmose III was old enough to become pharaoh. But she had herself crowned and, for a time, she was pharaoh in her own right.

## Akhenaten
REIGNED: 1352–1336 BCE
FAMOUS FOR: banishing the gods
This pharaoh worshipped Aten, the god represented by the disk of the Sun. He named himself Akhenaten ("glory of the Sun-disk") and founded a new capital city called Akhetaten. There, a new, less formal style of art developed. Akhenaten abandoned the old gods and closed their temples. He wanted people to worship only one god—Aten.

## Tutankhamun
REIGNED: 1336–1327 BCE
FAMOUS FOR: his burial treasures
A minor pharaoh who became king at the age of 9, he was Akhenaten's son. Tutankhamun changed Egypt's religion back to the worship of many gods. In 1922, his tomb was found in the Valley of the Kings with most treasures intact.

## Ramesses II
REIGNED: 1279–1213 BCE
FAMOUS FOR: buildings and battles
Known as Ramesses the Great, his 67-year reign is marked by the building of temples and statues and by a famous battle against the Hittites. The Battle of Qadesh (c.1274 BCE), in modern-day Syria, was inconclusive, and Ramesses signed the world's first peace treaty. He had more than 100 children.

## Queen Cleopatra VII
REIGNED: 51–30 BCE
FAMOUS FOR: being the last pharaoh
When Cleopatra VII became pharaoh, her family, the Ptolemies, had ruled Egypt for about 250 years. They were Greeks, not native Egyptians. Cleopatra ruled Egypt with help from the Romans. She killed herself by making a snake bite her, after which Egypt became part of the Roman Empire.

# THE MAIN GODS

## Amun, Amun-Ra
GOD OF: creation; king of the gods
LOOKS LIKE: a man wearing a crown with two tall feathered plumes
Became the supreme god during the New Kingdom and was worshipped throughout Egypt. His greatest temple was at Karnak. His name means Hidden or Invisible One.

## Anubis
GOD OF: embalming
LOOKS LIKE: a jackal or a jackal-headed man
According to myth, it was Anubis who wrapped the body of the murdered Osiris. It was because of this that he became associated with mummification.

## Aten
GOD OF: creation and light
LOOKS LIKE: the disk of the Sun whose rays ended in human hands
This sun god rose to prominence during the reign of Akhenaten. Aten's popularity only lasted a few years, and when Akhenaten died, people lost interest in this god.

## Bastet
GODDESS OF: joy; the home; the warmth of the Sun
LOOKS LIKE: domestic cat or a woman with the head of a cat
The center of her cult was at Bast, a town to the northeast of Cairo, where a great temple was built in her honor. Large cemeteries of mummified cats have been found close to her temple.

## Horus
GOD OF: the sky; the rising Sun; eternal life; keeper of order
LOOKS LIKE: a falcon or a man with the head of a falcon
He was the son of Osiris and Isis and was closely identified with the living pharaoh. His name means the Distant One.

## Isis
GODDESS OF: magic; wisdom; motherhood
LOOKS LIKE: a woman with the hieroglyph for her name (a throne) on her head
A caring mother goddess, Isis was sister and wife to Osiris and mother of Horus. She had great magical powers, which she used to bring her murdered husband back to life.

## Khepri
GOD OF: the rising Sun; creation
LOOKS LIKE: a scarab beetle or man with the head of a beetle
As a scarab beetle rolls a ball of dung along, Khepri was thought to push the sun up through the morning sky. Because he brought about the daily birth of the sun, he was also a god of creation.

## Khnum
GOD OF: the Nile in flood; pottery
LOOKS LIKE: A ram or a man with the head of a ram
Khnum was the god who made the Nile flood every year, leaving behind fertile soil. His link to soil made him a god of pottery.

## Nut

GODDESS OF: the sky and stars
LOOKS LIKE: a woman stretching
her body over the earth
The sky goddess Nut was the
wife and brother of Geb, the earth
god. Their children were Osiris,
Isis, and Seth.

## Osiris

GOD OF: the afterlife; the dead;
the fertile land
LOOKS LIKE: a green-faced mummy
wearing a crown of ostrich feathers
He was the husband and the brother
of Isis and the father of Horus.
Osiris was the first king to survive
death and became the ruler of the
afterlife, where he kept order among
those who journeyed there. He
bore the regalia of a king—the
crook and flail.

## Ra, Re

GOD OF: creation; father of the gods
LOOKS LIKE: a man with the head
of a hawk (or a ram) wearing a
Sun-disk headdress
Ra was the most important god in
ancient Egypt. He was a Sun god
who was worshipped from the
beginning of Egyptian history.
Every ruler called himself or herself
the "Son of Ra." It was believed that
after a pharaoh died, he joined Ra
in the heavens, traveling with him
through the skies in a solar barque
(Sun boat).

## Sekhmet

GOD OF: war
LOOKS LIKE: a lioness or a woman
with the head of a lioness
The goddess of warfare, Sekhmet

was thought to lead Egyptian armies
into battle. Her name means "she
who is powerful."

## Seth

GOD OF: chaos; storms; evil
LOOKS LIKE: an unidentified animal
with a narrow, curved snout and
long, rectangular ears
He was the brother of Osiris, whom
he murdered, and for this reason, he
was seen as the bringer of bad luck.
He was referred to as the "lord of
deserts and foreign lands."

## Sobek

GOD OF: fertility; strength; the Sun
LOOKS LIKE: a hippo or a man with a
hippo's head
Originally a god of strength, Sobek
later took on the features of other
gods, including Amun and Ra. As
Sobek-Ra, he was another version
of the sun god.

## Thoth

GOD OF: wisdom; writing, reading,
and mathematics; magic
LOOKS LIKE: a baboon, an ibis, or
a man with the head of an ibis
The god of scribes, Thoth is usually
shown holding a reed pen and a
writing palette. The ibis may have
been his symbol because its long,
curved beak looked like a pen. He
was the inventor of writing and
language. He was also the moon
god, which meant he controlled the
calendar and time itself.

# GLOSSARY

*Akh*
The part of a person's identity believed to live in the afterlife, formed when the *ba* and the *ka* were reunited.

**Amulet**
Object used as a protective device or lucky charm to ward off evil.

**Ankh**
Hieroglyph for the word meaning "life," shaped like a cross with a looped head.

*Ba*
A person's spirit or soul, thought to live on after death. The *ba* is often shown as a human-headed bird.

**Book of the Dead**
Collection of about 200 spells that were placed with the mummy to help the dead person reach the afterlife safely.

**Canopic jars**
Four jars that held the mummified stomach, liver, lungs, and intestines of a dead person.

**Cartonnage**
Material made from linen stiffened with plaster that was used to make mummy masks and coffins.

**Coffin**
Container in which a mummified body was placed, usually made from wood or cartonnage.

**Coffinette**
Small coffin in the shape of the mummy inside it, such as an animal.

**Crown**
Item of regalia worn by the pharaoh to symbolize his rule over Egypt. There were several different crowns.

**Demotic**
Style of handwriting that developed from the hieratic script and that could be written quickly.

*Deshret*
Name the ancient Egyptians called the desert that lay beyond their land. It meant "Red Land," after the color of the sand.

**Dynasty**
Series of pharaohs from related families. Egypt's pharaohs formed 31 dynasties.

**Emmer**
Type of wheat commonly grown in ancient Egypt.

**Faience**
Material formed from a paste of crushed quartz which had a glazed surface. It was fired hard in a kiln and was used to make small objects such as amulets.

**Hieratic**
Form of handwriting that was developed from hieroglyphs and was quick to write.

**Hieroglyphs**
The oldest writing script used in ancient Egypt, consisting of signs that refer to the meaning and sound of words.

**Inundation**
The period when the River Nile flooded each year—between June and September.

*Ka*
Life force or "double" of a living person formed at birth. After death, the *ka* lived in the dead person's tomb, where it survived, provided there were offerings left there for it.

**Kemet**
Ancient Egyptian name for Egypt. It meant "Black Land," after the color of the mud deposited by the River Nile when it flooded.

**Lapis lazuli**
Highly prized dark blue stone from Afghanistan used in ancient Egypt for amulets and jewelry.

**Lower Egypt**
The northern region of ancient Egypt.

**Mastaba**
Rectangular bench-shaped tomb with a flat roof.

**Mummy**
Preserved body. In ancient Egypt, human and animal bodies were artificially mummified by drying them out with natron, then wrapping with linen bandages.

**Natron**
A type of salt that occurred naturally in Egypt and was used to dry bodies during the process of mummification.

**Obelisk**
Tall stone with a pyramid-shaped top that was a symbol of the Sun's rays.

**Opening of the Mouth**
Ceremony performed on mummies to restore them to life.

**Papyrus**
Water reed used to make a type of writing paper, baskets, ropes, sandals, and medicine. Its root could be eaten or burned as fuel.

**Pharaoh**
Ruler of ancient Egypt.

**Pyramid**
Tomb with a square base and four sloping sides, built to hold the mummified body of a pharaoh.

**Saqqara**
Burial ground near Memphis (south of Cairo) that was used for royal and private burials.

**Sarcophagus**
Stone coffin. The word is from the Greek for "flesh eater."

**Scribe**
Person trained to read and write.

**Sed festival**
Festival for renewing a pharaoh's divine strength, which was held in the 30th year of his reign.

**Senet**
Board game similar to today's game of checkers, played on a board of 30 squares.

**Sidelock of youth**
Long lock of hair on children who were not yet old enough to be thought of as adults.

**Sphinx**
Creature with a lion's body and human head, particularly that of the pharaoh.

**Thebes**
Capital of Egypt during the New Kingdom.

**Upper Egypt**
The southern region of ancient Egypt.

**Valley of the Kings**
Burial site used during the New Kingdom for the burial of pharaohs in rock-cut tombs.

**Vizier**
The chief ministers and the highest officials in the government. They kept the king informed on all matters.

**Weighing of the Heart**
When a dead person's heart was weighed against a feather to see if they were worthy of entering the afterlife.

# INDEX

# ACKNOWLEDGMENTS

**Dorling Kindersley would like to thank:**
Almudena Diaz and Nomazwe Modonko for DTP assistance.
Thanks also to Chris Bernstein for the index.

**Picture Credits**
The publisher would like to thank the following for their kind permission to reproduce their images:
Key: a-above; b-below/bottom; c-center; f-far; l-left; r-right; t-top

**Owen Beattie:**
University of Alberta, 11br

**Bolton Museum:**
10bl

**Bridgeman Art Library, London/New York:**
David Roberts, City of Bristol Museum and Art Gallery, 59; Giraudon/Louvre, Paris, France, 7; 63

**British Museum:**
3, 21t, 22b, 23b, 24tr, 24bl, 26l, 27c, 28l, 30bl, 31b, 33c, 34b, 36tl, 36b, 38tl, 39b, 42tl, 43b, 49br, 55, 56–57, 58, 61bc, 62tl, 64tl, 65, 70c, 74c, 74bl, 77, 78, 79, 80cl, 80t, 81, 82b, 83, 84; Peter Hayman, 1, 8tl

**Cairo Museum:**
6, 48c

**Corbis:**
Richard T. Nowitz, 16bl; Sygma, 35br; Sygma/Viennareport Agency, 8b

**Alistair Duncan, Egyptian Museum Cairo:** 14cr, 17tr, 19c, 25b, 29c, 50c, 51tr, 53, 67tr, 68b;

**Mary Evans Picture Library:**
49t

**Werner Forman Archive:**
44cl; Egyptian Museum Cairo, 54

**Ronald Grant Archive:**
13cr

**Jurgen Liepe:**
66b

**Manchester Museum:**
20bc, 30cr, 52, 72t

**NASA:**
15c

**Science Photo Library:**
Geoff Tompkinson, 12tr; John Sandford, 45tr

**Silkeborg Museum, Denmark:**
9tr

**Getty Images, Stone:**
Richard Passmore, 60–61

All other images © Dorling Kindersley.

For further information see:
**www.dkimages.com**